CONTEMPORARY

SQUARE

DANCE

Sandra J. Stultz

Ball State University
Muncie, Indiana

Burgess Publishing Company
Minneapolis, Minnesota

Dedication

To my parents, whose love, time, and
patience made my knowledge possible.

Contents

Foreword

Twenty-five years ago there existed a close correlation between square dancing taught in the public schools and colleges when compared to public square dancing at the recreational level. This comparison would be universally valid throughout most of the square dance world. The square dancing to the end of World War II was largely visiting couple type dancing with close association to the form, call, and style which originated with those early American settlers who evolved the dance.

In more recent years the square dance at the public recreational level has changed drastically in the form, call, costume, amplification, workshop, and music areas which constitute the activity. In our educational institutions, change in teacher preparation for square dance leadership has become evident to some extent, but most individuals who learn square dance in schools today are still exposed to the type of dancing which is a part of our distant past. It is called square dancing, but it is not contemporary.

This book represents an effort to place materials in a workable form for use as a basis for teaching students the rudiments of contemporary square dancing at the college level. This is a "first" in the square dance teaching area. The book does an outstanding job of placing the square dance material in a very acceptable form for use in a teacher preparation program. It should serve as a guide to those who are interested in pursuing or developing a program of square dance.

It would be my hope that this book would stimulate students to utilize the Western square dance approach to teaching in the public schools and also that colleges and universities who are unfamiliar with the contemporary square dance form would develop interests at least to an exploratory degree which would bring about evaluation of its possible implications for the square dance programs of America.

Fall, 1974   James Hedge
                                          Indiana Dancers Association
                                          Professional Caller

Preface

   This book is intended for all people who enjoy square dancing. Those people who are learning to square dance as well as those people teaching square dance. It deals with the very basic aspects to the more difficult aspects of square dance and the calling of square dance.

   The book's basic purpose is to show easy-to-learn skills and easy-to-teach instruction of modern techniques of square dance in a progressive sequence. It can also be used as a textbook for square dance classes or as a reference guide for skills learned.

   No attempt has been made to list every record company or record store available, but the lists prepared would be sufficient to start or conduct a square dance group. The lists provided are: Record Company Bibliography; Dress, Equipment, and Record Sources; Square Dance Associations; and Books and Magazines Bibliography.

   For the caller and instructor of square dance, the book's format is presented in a series form (three to ten calls per series) to aid the instructor and caller in teaching the calls in a progressive, logical, and flowing sequence. Patter calling, a recent trend in modern square dance, is considered a major part of the text and follows every series of calls. Also, singing call suggestions are given after every series which include the title of the record, the record company, and the record number for easy reference and ordering from the Record Company Bibliography located in the Appendix.

   It is the author's wish that her book will be of help and inspiration to the many square dance enthusiasts throughout the nation.

Acknowledgments

The author wishes to express special thanks to the following people:

To Dr. Ruth Andrews, Retired Head of the Women's Physical Education Department, Ball State University, Muncie, Indiana, for her encouragement and direction in the area of square dance.

To Dr. Jean Arrasmith, Head of the Women's Physical Education Department, Ball State University, Muncie, Indiana, for her continued support.

To her colleagues, Dr. Cecile Gilbert, Dr. Rosemary Fisher, Dr. Adelaide Cole, Dr. Patricia Brown, Dr. Janice Stocker, Nancy Linson, Coranell Rossow, Elaine Estes, Leslie Lampen, Yaakev Eden, and Jean Smith, for their advice and cooperation.

To the Ball State University students who expressed their confidence, enthusiasm, and skill in their dance classes. A special thanks to Diana Stevens, a former student, for her assistance in compiling the book.

To the Indiana Dancers Association and Mr. James Hedge, a professional square dance caller, for their incentive.

Sandra J. Stultz

Symbols

The following symbols were used to designate the fundamental movements:

☐ Man

◯ Lady

Arrow shows the way the man faces.

Arrow shows the way the lady faces.

Couples have right hands joined.

Couples have left hands joined.

Couples have nearest hands joined.
   Man's right and lady's left hand.

Couples have both hands joined.

Movement in a clockwise direction.

Movement in a counterclockwise direction.

Preliminary Language

Couple: A man and his lady partner.

Square: A square consists of an arrangement of four couples who stand facing the center in a square formation. The four positions designate the
couples' home positions.

Couples 1-2-3-4: Couples are numbered consecutively to the right starting
with couple number one, who have their backs to the music.

Head Couples: Number one and number three couples.

Side Couples: Number two and number four couples.

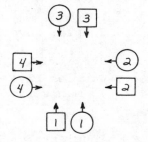

Partner: Lady is on the right of the man.

Corner: Lady is on the left of the man.

Right Hand Lady: The lady in the couple on the right.
Opposite: The couple directly across the square.

   The following diagram shows the above positions in relationship to
number one man.

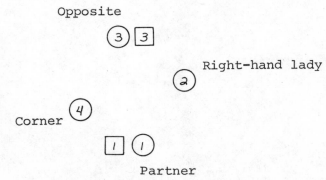

Forming Sets

1. Grand March--Men are assembled in a single file line on one side of the
   room, facing the caller and music. The ladies are on the opposite side of
   the room in a single file line, facing the caller and music. As the music
   begins, each line moves towards the caller and the center of the room.
   When the two lines meet, they join hands with the partner they meet and
   march down the center of the room forming one long line of couples. From
   the line, the first four couples break away and form a set. The next four
   couples do the same until all the couples in the line are in a set.

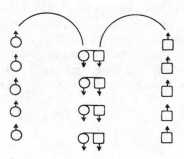

2. Grand March II--The preliminary assembly of the men and ladies is in the
   same manner as described in the Grand March in number one. When the
   couples are formed in one long line down the center of the room, you continue the Grand March by having each couple separate alternately by going
   left and right. They continue their march to the head of the room and meet
   another couple. The group of four then proceeds down the center of the
   room until they reach the end. The Grand March is again continued by alternately separating each group of four left and right. The groups of
   four march around the room to the head and join with the group of four
   they meet and form groups of eight. The groups of eight continue down
   the center of the room until they reach the end. The groups of eight then
   separate alternately left and right to form sets.

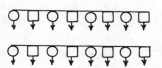

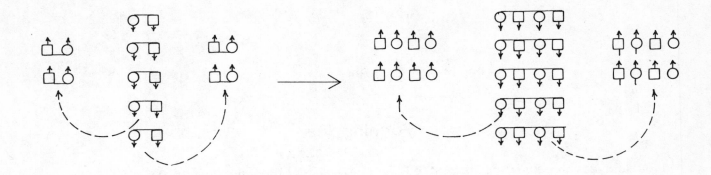

3. Circle Formation--Preliminary assembly of men and ladies is in the same manner as the Grand March described in number one. When couples are formed in one long line down the center of the room the line is stopped momentarily. The caller then instructs each man to step in front of his partner to form one single line. The dancers then face a quarter turn to the right and all join hands. The caller leads the line of dancers in a clockwise direction around the room until they reach the opposite end and form a large circle. In the large circle formation, the man's partner is on his right and his corner is on his left. Calls such as: Honor your partner, Circle left and right, Do-sa-do your partner, See-Saw your corner, Allemande left your corner, Allemande right your partner, Swing your partner, Promenade your partner.

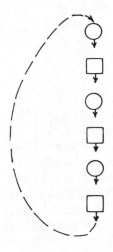

From the large circle formation, two variations can be used to place the dancers into sets.

   A. Sicilian Circle--Place the dancers in promenade position in the
      large circle formation facing counterclockwise. Then alternate
      couples in this formation wheel around, gent keeping his partner on
      his right (turn around), and face the couple directly behind them.
      Calls such as two ladies chain, right and left through, circle four
      can be introduced. From the circle four formation, the caller then
      instructs the dancers to break at one spot (DO NOT MAKE THE BREAK

BETWEEN PARTNERS) and find another group of four and circle up eight. From the group of eight the dancers form sets.

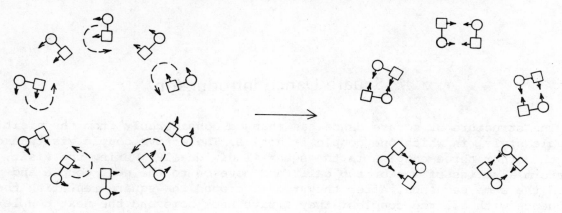

B. **Scatter Promenade**--Place the dancers in promenade position in the large circle formation facing counterclockwise. The caller then instructs the dancers to scatter promenade in any direction around the room without bumping into another couple. At the caller's command, each couple finds another couple and they circle up four. From the circle four formation, they break at one spot (DO NOT MAKE THE BREAK BETWEEN PARTNERS) and find another group of four and circle up eight. From the group of eight the dancers form sets.

Square Dance Introduction

The structure of square dance has changed considerably from the visiting couple style, in which one couple is active. The active couple visits each of the other three couples in the square individually. During the visit, they perform a series of one or two calls and move on to the next couple and perform the same sequence. After they travel around the square repeating the sequence with all the couples, they arrive back home and the next couple starts their visits around the square. Every couple in the square follows the same pattern in sequence.

Contemporary square dance, the style used by most groups today, involves two active couples (heads or sides), and the remaining two couples (inactive) are considered POSTS in which the active couples go in, out, and around in the set. The inactive couples must stay alert, however, because they need to separate many times and let the active couples pass through them. The inactive couples also perform calls with the active couples throughout the dance.

Recreational square dance has grown greatly since the transition from the visiting style (one active couple) to contemporary style (two active couples). Square dancing develops skill and knowledge of calls, mental alertness, coordination, rhythm, agility, gracefulness, and endurance. People enjoy the social aspect of square dance--meeting new friends at square dances. Square dancing provides a challenge to all ages and can be enjoyed as a lifetime activity.

Square Dance Calling

There are two methods of calling currently used in square dance: patter calls (hash or chant call) and singing calls.

Patter calls are when the caller directs the dancers without reference to any predetermined sequence. The caller must know a vast number of calls and the relationship of these calls to each other. The caller must thoroughly understand the movements in order to determine where the dancers will end and whether the next call can be executed. The caller builds one call onto another until the couples are back in their home positions. The dancers must listen very carefully to the caller and must be alert enough to respond. Patter calling adds an element of surprise which presents a challenge to the dancers' skills. Patter calling is much harder to learn but a greater satisfaction is felt both by the caller and the dancers.

A *singing call* means that the commands or directions given follow the melody of a particular song. Singing call dances usually follow a particular pattern. The basic pattern of most singing calls is: introduction, main figure (heads), break, main figure (sides), and ending. The introduction, break, and ending usually contain the same figure with no partner change. The main figure has a partner change and needs to be repeated four times (twice for the heads and twice for the sides) in order for the dancers to end up in their original positions with original partners.

The techniques of square dance calling are as follows.

1. You must learn to enunciate clearly so that the dancers can understand the command. The key words are emphasized, such as MEN star RIGHT; ALLE-MANDE LEFT and the MEN star RIGHT. Sharp cue words are important.

2. Caller should give all the verbal help he can without being wordy. Example: *Back to the corner* for an allemande left instead of just saying allemande left.

3. Allow time for the dancers to execute the commands. It is better to have the dancers wait than to call too fast.

4. The caller must call within the framework of the dancers' knowledge.

5. The caller should be at least one call ahead of the dancers.

6. The caller must be aware of the beat at all times. The records usually contain sixty-four beats, and the caller should listen for the accumulative phrasing of four, eight, sixteen, thirty-two, and sixty-four beats and make changes in action in relation to the phrases.

7. The caller should avoid calling two movements with the same hand or side. For example, if the call is allemande left, the following call should be done with the right hand or side. Example: allemande left and the men star right or allemande left the corner and do-sa-do partner.

8. The caller should avoid using cue cards because his eyes should be kept on the dancers.

Techniques of Performance

Listed below are some suggestions for the dancers to follow for better results.

1. Remind the dancers to never try and outguess the caller. The dancers must not anticipate the calls.

2. The dancers should be discouraged from clapping and stomping because the dancers need to hear the calls and concentrate on the movements.

3. When the square gets lost, instruct the dancers to return to their home positions and wait for the next call when they can start again.

4. Change sets occasionally. This gives the dancers a feeling of performing skills with relationships to new sets and new partners.

5. The dancers should counterbalance the movements with each other. Hands and arms should not be limp. The dancers need to feel the movement in order to get the full benefit from square dancing.

6. The dancers should be encouraged to form sets quickly, usually when the music starts or at caller's command. Couples in a set can aid the caller in filling sets by indicating with their hands how many additional couples are needed to fill their set.

7. Once you have a complete set, the dancers should square the set. This is done by extending arms out at shoulder level, touching fingertips with the corner.

8. Never leave a set idle by walking away. Always find a couple to replace you if you need to leave a set.

Outline of Beginning Series

SERIES I
- A. Shuffle Step
- B. Honor
- C. Circle to Left and Right
- D. Promenade
  - 1. couple
  - 2. single file
  - 3. half
  - 4. inside and outside
  - 5. ladies and men
- E. Do-sa-do
- F. See-Saw
- G. Allemande Left and Right
- H. Grand Right and Left

Series I Patter Calls

<u>Suggested Singing Calls for Series I</u>

Oh! Johnny!--MacGregor #652A

SERIES II
- A. Ladies Chain
  - 1. two ladies
  - 2. four ladies (grand chain)
  - 3. three-quarters ladies chain
- B. All around Left Hand Lady
- C. Rollaway-Half Sashay
- D. Whirlaway
- E. Weave the Ring
- F. Right and Left Thru

Series II Patter Calls

<u>Suggested Singing Calls for Series II</u>

Bumming Around--Golden Square #6004
Alabama Jubilee--MacGregor #638 A
         (With Calls)
      MacGregor #640 B
       (Without)
If You Knew Susie--Blue Star #1600
Just Because--Windsor #4444 (With Calls)
      Windsor #4144 (Without)
Yes Sir, That's My Baby--MacGregor
        #655 B

SERIES III
- A. Star
  - 1. ladies or gents
  - 2. right or left
- B. Back by Right or Left
- C. Star Promenade
- D. Ladies to the Center and Back to Bar
- E. Turn by Left or Right

Series III Patter Calls

<u>Suggested Singing Calls for Series III</u>

Chime Bells--Top #25174
Four Leaf Clover--Bogan #1136
Little Ole Winemaker--Kalox #K-1086
Marina--Grenn #2140

SERIES IV
    A. Pass Thru
    B. California or Frontier Twirl
    C. Dive Thru
    D. Star Thru
    E. Split the Ring
    F. Separate Go Around One or Two

Series IV Patter Calls

Suggested Singing Calls for Series IV

Dime a Dozen--Blue Star #1676
Everybody Loves a Lover--MacGregor
                        #8925
Gentle on My Mind--Wagon Wheel #113
Jambalaya--Top #25032
Proud Mary--Kalox #K-1116
Winchester Cathedral--Grenn #12088

SERIES V
    A. Circle to a Line
    B. Bend the Line
    C. Wheel Around
    D. Crosstrail

Series V Patter Calls

Suggested Singing Calls for Series V

Amapola--Top #25030
April Showers--Blue Star #1604
Five Foot Two--Square Your Sets #1001
Goodbye Lady Love--Top #25096
Tipperary--Balance #X110

SERIES VI
    A. Substitute
    B. Box the Gnat
    C. Box the Flea

Series VI Patter Calls

Suggested Singing Calls for Series VI

It's Later Than You Think--Keeno #2150
Let's Go Back to Donegal--Top #25036
Little Arrows--Top #25186
Mary Ann--Windsor #4815
Ragtime Piano--Windsor #4803
There'll Be Some Changes Made--Blue
    Star #1631
Yes, Sir--Old Timer #8177

SERIES VII
    A. Grand Square
    B. Square Thru
        1. full
        2. half
        3. three-quarters

Series VII Patter Calls

Suggested Singing Calls for Series VII

Are You from Dixie--Sets in Order #124
Chewing Gum--Go #104
June Night--Sets in Order #F102
Lady Be Good--Grenn #12043
Ragtime Banjo Ball--Top #25035
The Possom Song--Blue Star #1630
Thunder Road--Windsor #4809
Wheels Q--Top #25075
When You're Swinging--Lore #1017

SERIES VIII
    A. Wheel and Deal
    B. Double Pass Thru
    C. Cloverleaf

Suggested Singing Calls for Series VIII

Big Daddy--Grenn #12035
Give My Regards to Broadway--Blue Star
                        #1623 .
King of the Road--Wagon Wheel #109
Mister Piano Man--MacGregor #1061
Old Black Magic--Hi Hat #339
Ride, Ride, Ride--Grenn #12093
Swinging Billie Joe--Wagon Wheel #108

Outline of Intermediate Series

SERIES IX
   A. Pair Off
   B. Ocean Wave
   C. Swing Thru
   D. Boys Trade
   E. Girls Trade

Patter Calls for Series IX

Suggested Singing Calls for Series IX

Everythin' Is Rosy Now--Lore #1019
Full Time Job--MacGregor #1001
Just in Time--Windsor #4889
Saturday Night--Jay Bar Kay #L5006
Six Days on the Road--Began #1160
That's Where My Baby Use to Be--Blue
                              Star #1820
Whispering--Balance #403
Wildflower--Scope #512
You Do Something to Me--Aqua #113

SERIES X
   A. Turn Thru
   B. Double Swing Thru
   C. Alamo Style Balance

Patter Calls for Series X

Suggested Singing Calls for Series X

Baby That's Living--Hi Hat #361
Baby Won't You Please Come Home--Kalox
                              #LH169
My Window Faces the South--Kalox #B-
                              115
Rink-A-Tink Piano--Top #25177
Sally Jane--Windsor #4898A
The Greatest--Windsor #4955
Yes, Yes--Windsor #4890

SERIES XI
   A. Slide Thru
   B. Partner.Trade
   C. Trade By

Patter Calls for Series XI

Suggested Singing Calls for Series XI

Snowbird--Hi Hat #397
Under the Sun--Top 325276
Wave Goodbye to Me--MacGregor #2035

SERIES XII
   A. Men Run
   B. Circulate Men
   C. Circulate Ladies
   D. All Eight Circulate
   E. Couples Circulate

Patter Calls for Series XII

Suggested Singing Calls for Series XII

No More No Less--Hi Hat #334
Pass Me By--MacGregor #1064
Ring of Fire--Jay Bar Kay #118

SERIES XVII
    A. Flutter Wheel
    B. Sweep a Quarter
    C. Tag the Line

Patter Calls for Series XVII

<u>Suggested Singing Calls for Series XVII</u>

Abilene--MacGregor #2106 B

SERIES XVIII
    A. Eight Chain Thru
    B. Catch All Eight

Patter Calls for Series XVIII

<u>Suggested Singing Calls for Series XVIII</u>

Can't Help Believing--Wagon Wheel #120
Gonna Raise a Ruckus--Windsor #4818
Hello My Baby--MacGregor #1008A
Just a Little Lovin'--Windsor #4889
L-O-V-E--Blue Star #1859
Pickle Up a Doodle--Windsor #4823
Rolling Along--Kalox #LH 4827
Sally Was a Good Ole Girl--Wagon Wheel
                             #307
Sweet Thang--Jewel #J-141
Tico Tico--Kalox #1017
Wishing--Sets in Order #119A

SERIES IXX
    A. Cast Off
    B. Centers In
    C. Center Out
    D. Fold

Patter Calls for Series IXX

<u>Suggested Singing Calls for Series IXX</u>

I'm Walkin'--Top #25123

SERIES XX
    A. Barge Thru

Patter Calls for Series XX

<u>Suggested Singing Calls for Series XX</u>

No No Nora--Scope #127

Shuffle
Honor
Buzz Step Swing
Circle to the Left/
Circle to the Right
Promenade
Do-sa-do
See-saw
Allemande Left/
Allemande Right
Grand Right and Left

Series I

SHUFFLE: The basic step used in square dancing. The dancers take tiny steps trying to keep their feet close to the floor, creating a shuffle sound.

HONOR: The men bow and the ladies curtsey.

BUZZ STEP SWING: The dancers are in closed dance position: man's left hand joined with lady's right hand and man's right arm is placed around the lady's waist while the lady's left hand is on the man's shoulder. The outside of the right foot of the two dancers is placed next to each other. The left foot of each of the two dancers is used to propel the body around in a clockwise direction. The couples need to counterbalance and lean away from each other. The dancers go once around using four counts, then the man places the lady on his right side in direction of the next call.

CIRCLE TO THE LEFT OR RIGHT: Designated couples join hands to form a circle and move clockwise to the left and counterclockwise to the right. If the caller does not designate right or left, the circle always moves to the left or clockwise.

PROMENADE
A. Couple: This is the basic promenade used in square dancing. The couples have their right hands joined and the left hands joined with the right hands on top of the left hands. Both hands are held waist high. The couples promenade in a counterclockwise direction. The man's left shoulder should be kept close to the center of the set to keep the promenade small. The couples promenade around and back to their home positions.

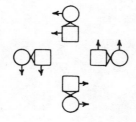

B. **Single File Promenade:** The couples promenade one behind the other in a single file. When moving left or clockwise the man is in the lead. When moving right or counterclockwise the lady is in the lead.

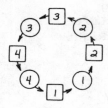 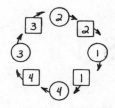

Lady Lead   Gent Lead

C. **Half Promenade:** The designated couples use the couple promenade position and move counterclockwise to exchange places. Eight counts.

D. **Inside or Outside Promenade:** This call usually goes with the call half promenade. The designated couples either promenade inside or outside of the other two couples. If the promenade is done outside of the other two couples, the couples should take two steps in and then out after the designated couples have passed.

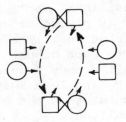 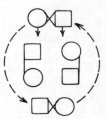

Inside   Outside

E. **Ladies Promenade or Men Promenade:** The ladies or men step toward the center and promenade around inside and back to their home position. The people indicated go in a counterclockwise direction.

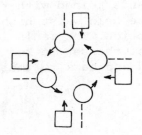 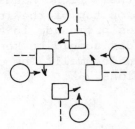

Lady   Gent

2

DO-SA-DO: Two dancers facing each other pass right shoulders, back to back, and then left shoulders. The two dancers move around each other without turning and back to place. Eight counts.

SEE-SAW: Two dancers facing each other pass left shoulders, back to back, and then right shoulders. The two dancers move around each other without turning and back to place. Eight counts.

ALLEMANDE LEFT OR RIGHT: Two persons holding hands, either right or left, walk around each other and back to place. Allemande left is usually done with the corner and is often followed by a right and left grand. Allemande right is usually done with the lady on the right or partner. Eight counts.

GRAND RIGHT AND LEFT: Partners face and take right hands. Each moves ahead to give left hand to the next, right to the next, left to the next, then meet your partner for the next call. The men always go counterclockwise and the ladies go clockwise around the set. The grand right and left usually follows an allemande left with the corner. Sixteen counts.

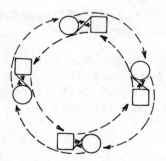

Patter Calls for Series I

Honor your partner, honor your corner
All join hands and circle to the left
Now circle to the right
Then swing your partner and promenade the ring.

Head two couples promenade half way around,
    inside the ring
Side couples do the same
Head couples promenade halfway around,
    outside the ring
Side couples do the same.

Promenade single file, lady in the lead
All turn back and promenade single file,
    men in the lead
Men turn around and swing your partner
Then promenade the ring.

Head two couples promenade all the way around
    outside the ring
Side couples do the same
Head two couples promenade all the way around
    inside the ring
Side couples do the same
Allemande left with the corner girl
Right to your partner for a right and left grand.
Meet your partner and promenade her home.

Join hands and circle to the left, drop hands and
    promenade single file, men in the lead
Join hands and circle to the right, drop hands and
    promenade single file, lady in the lead
Ladies turn around, swing your partner and promenade home.

All four ladies promenade inside the ring, get back home
    and swing your partner
All four gents promenade inside the ring, get back home
    and swing your partner
Allemande left with your left hand
Right to your partner for a right and left grand
Meet your partner and promenade her home.

Allemande left your corner, do-sa-do your partner
Back to the corner with an allemande left
Right to your partner for a right and left grand
Then promenade eight when you come straight.

4

All join hands and circle eight
Face the corner and do an allemande left
Face your partner and do an allemande right
Go back to the corner--allemande left
Do-sa-do your partner and promenade.

Head couples promenade halfway around; inside the ring
Side couples do the same
Then join hands and circle to the left
Face the corner--see-saw
Back to your partner for a do-sa-do
Allemande left with the corner, promenade partner.

All join hands and circle left
Face the partner and do an allemande right
See-saw the corner and back to partner for an
    allemande right
Allemande left with the corner and promenade
    partner home.

See-saw your corner, allemande right with partner
Allemande left with corner, then do a grand ole right and left
Meet your partner and do a do-sa-do
Turn to the corner and see-saw
Swing your partner and promenade right.

All join hands and circle left
Swing that ole partner and promenade the ring
Honor your partner, honor your corner
Wave to the people across the hall
That's all!

Four ladies promenade inside the ring, back to your partner
    and swing
Four men promenade inside the ring, back to your partner
    and do an allemande right.
Allemande left with your left hand
Back home and swing your partner and promenade the ring.

Recommended Singing Calls for Series I

Oh! Johnny!
    MacGregor: Number 652A (With Calls)
    Folkraft: Number 1037 (Without Calls)

CALLS INCLUDED IN SERIES II

Ladies Chain
All Around Left Hand Lady
Rollaway-Half Sashay
Whirlaway
Weave the Ring
Right and Left Thru

Series II

LADIES CHAIN

A. Two Ladies Chain: Two ladies indicated give right hands to each other, pull by passing right shoulders, giving left hand to the opposite man in his left hand. The man then turns the lady around by backing up and the lady walks forward. The men should step in to meet the lady as she is chaining. The ladies chain can be done over and back, but the ladies do not return unless the caller indicates such. Eight counts.

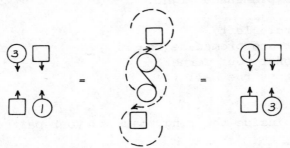

B. Four Ladies Chain or Grand Chain: All four ladies advance toward the center of the set. The ladies extend their right hands up to each other and move clockwise to the opposite man. The men then turn the ladies in place. The grand chain back would repeat the action and return the ladies to their starting positions. Eight counts.

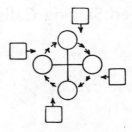

C. Three-Quarters Ladies Chain: All four ladies advance toward the center of the set. The ladies extend their right hands up to each other and move clockwise, passing two positions and ending with the lady's corner.

6

The men then turn the ladies in place. Twelve counts.

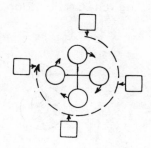

ALL AROUND LEFT HAND LADY: The left hand lady is another name for the
    corner. The man and lady move towards each other without turning and the
    man goes behind the lady and then in front and back to place. Both the
    man and the lady remain facing the center of the set and move around each
    other using side steps. Eight counts.

ROLLAWAY HALF SASHAY: Couples are in a circle or square formation. The man
    using his right hand, the lady's left hand, pulls the lady across in
    front. The lady makes a full turn across in front of the man. The result
    is that the two have exchanged places. Four counts.

WHIRLAWAY: The ladies indicated make a full turn under the man's raised right
    arm turning counterclockwise. The lady remains on the same side as when
    she started (partner's right side). Four counts.

WEAVE THE RING: This is a grand right and left without touching hands.
    For styling, the men place both hands on their hips and the ladies hold
    out their skirts. Sixteen counts.

RIGHT AND LEFT THRU: Executed while two couples are facing each other. Each
    person goes towards the person in front joining right hands. Then the
    couples pull by, passing right shoulders, and giving a left hand to part-
    ner in his left hand. The men then turn the ladies around in place by

backing up and the ladies moving forward. This turn is referred to as a courtesy turn, the result being that the couple ends across from where they started.

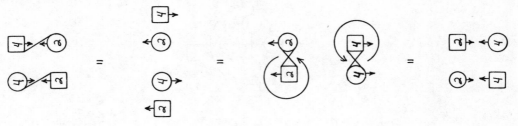

Patter Calls for Series II

Head couples do a right and left thru
Side couples do a right and left thru
Allemande left your corner lady
Do-sa-do your own and promenade home.

Four ladies chain, three-quarters, circle to the left
Four ladies rollaway, circle to the left.
Allemande left the corner and promenade partner home.

Four ladies chain across, join hands and circle to the left
Four ladies rollaway, circle to the left
Four ladies rollaway, circle to the left
Allemande left corner, right hand to partner
    for a right and left grand.
Meet your partner and promenade her home.

Join hands and circle to the left, allemande left
    the corner girl and promenade partner.
Head couples promenade halfway outside the ring
Down the middle and do a right and left thru
Allemande left your corner, do-sa-do your own.
Four ladies chain three-quarters, circle to the left
Four ladies rollaway and circle to the left
Allemande left your corner girl and promenade partner home.

Head couples go forward and do a right and left thru
Side couples do the same
Head couples do a right and left back
Side couples do the same.
Allemande left with the corner and weave the ring.
Do-sa-do with partner when you meet
Join hands and circle to the left
Go all around your left hand lady and promenade partner home.

Two head ladies chain over
Two side ladies chain over
Two head ladies chain back
Two side ladies chain back
Join hands and circle--walk all around the left hand lady
See-saw partners all
Allemande left with corner gal and weave that big ole ring
Promenade partner when you meet.

The two head ladies chain over, two side ladies chain over
All four ladies chain three-quarters
Then join hands and circle to the right, drop hands a go single file
Men turn around and swing ole partner--she's on the corner
Then promenade the ring.

Four ladies chain across the ring, turn 'em men
Four ladies chain three-quarters
Join hands and circle to the left, face the corner
    and swing
Promenade her home.

Four ladies chain three-quarters, four ladies chain three-quarters
Four ladies chain across and join hands, circle to the left
Walk around the left hand lady, do-sa-do with partner
Allemande left with the corner and weave the ring.
Meet partner and promenade her home.

Four ladies chain across the ring,
Chain them back in the same ole track
Join hands and circle to the left
Four ladies whirlaway and circle to the left
Walk around the corner and promenade partner home.

Recommended Singing Calls for Series II

Bumming Around
    Golden Square: Number 6004

Alabama Jubilee
    MacGregor: Number 638A (With Calls)
                Number 640B (Without Calls)

If you Knew Susie
    Blue Star: Number 1600

Just Because
    Windsor: Number 4444 (With Calls)
              Number 4144 (Without Calls)

Yes Sir, That's My Baby
    MacGregor: Number 655B

Series III

CALLS INCLUDED IN SERIES III

Stars
Back by left or right
Turn by the right or left
Star promenade
Ladies to center and back
Backtrack

STAR: The men place their right or left side toward the center of the set and take hold of the man's wrist in front of him with hand on top. The four men form a small box and move in the designated direction. Ladies hold hands and form a star in the center of the set. The ladies put the designated hand out touching fingers together and move either clockwise or counterclockwise.

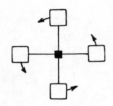

BACK BY THE LEFT OR RIGHT: Those in the star release the hold, make a half right or left face turn, and form the star moving in the opposite direction.

STAR PROMENADE: Formed from a man's star, the men place their free arm around their partner's waist while still holding on to the star. The star continues to move. The women have their closest arm on the man's shoulder closest to her.

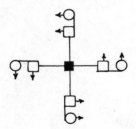

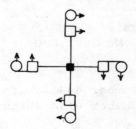

LADIES TO THE CENTER AND BACK TO THE BAR: Those ladies indicated take two
steps into the center of the set and two steps back to home positions.
Four counts.

BACKTRACK: This call can be done from a star promenade or a single file
promenade. The ladies turn out from the promenade and walk once around in
the opposite direction until the next call.

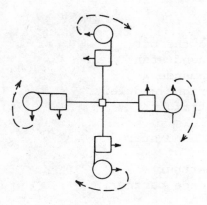

Backtrack from
Left Hand Star
Promenade

Backtrack from Single File Promenade

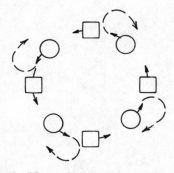

Ladies in the Lead

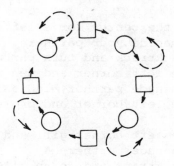

Men in the Lead

TURN BY THE LEFT OR RIGHT: Two persons holding forearms, either turn right
or left by walking around each other and back to place. Eight counts.

Patter Calls for Series III

Ladies to the center and back to the bar
    into the middle and form a right hand star
Back by the left
Turn your partner by the right
All the way around to the corner for an allemande left
Back to your partner and do-sa-do
Promenade partner home.

Ladies to the center and back to the bar
    into the center for a right hand star
Go to the corner for a left allemande
Go to your partner for a grand right and left
Promenade eight when you come straight.

Men into the center with a left hand star
Star promenade partner
Ladies backtrack and do-sa-do partner
Allemande left corner and promenade partner.

Men into the center for a left hand star
Star promenade partner
Ladies backtrack and go twice around
Meet partner and do-sa-do
Allemande left corner and weave the ring
Promenade partner.

Men into the center for a left hand star
Star promenade your partner
Ladies backtrack and turn partner by the right
Allemande left corner and men star right
Star promenade partner, ladies backtrack
Allemande left corner and promenade partner home.

Allemande left corner girl and men star right
Star promenade partner
Ladies backtrack and do an allemande left corner
Give a right to partner for a grand right and left
Do-sa-do partner and the men star left
Star promenade partner
Ladies backtrack, do-sa-do partner and promenade home.

Ladies to the center and back to the bar
Ladies form a right hand star
Back by the left, turn partner by the right
Corner by the left and the men star right
Star promenade partner
Ladies backtrack, allemande left corner and promenade partner.

Ladies to the center and back to the bar
Ladies form a right hand star
Back by the left
Do-sa-do partner, allemande left corner
Men star right, back by the left
Star promenade partner
Ladies backtrack twice around
Turn partner by the right, allemande left corner
Right to partner for a right and left grand
Promenade partner.

Allemande left the corner girl
Men star right, back by the left
Star promenade partner
Ladies backtrack and do-sa-do partner
Girls star left and back by the right
Turn corner by the left and partner by the right
Men star left.
Star promenade partner
Ladies backtrack, do-sa-do partner
Allemande left the corner and promenade partner.

Recommended Singing Calls for Series III

Chime Bells
    Top: Number 25174

Four Leaf Clover
    Bogan: Number 1136

Little Ole Winemaker
    Kalox: Number K-1086

Marina
    Grenn: Number 12140

CALLS INCLUDED IN SERIES IV

Pass thru
California twirl
Dive thru
Star thru
Split the ring
Separate and go around one, two

Series IV

PASS THRU: Two couples facing each other go forward and pass right shoulders.
   The couples then face the outside of the set and wait for the next call.
   Count four.

CALIFORNIA TWIRL: Another name for the California twirl is the frontier
   whirl. It is done automatically when two dancers are facing away from the
   center of the set. The call is used when the couples need to get back facing
   the center of the set. The call is done with the man's right and lady's left
   hand. The man walks around in front of the lady, while the lady turns counterclockwise under the man's raised right arm. The result is that the two people
   who were facing out are now facing back in toward the center of the set. Four
   counts.

DIVE THRU: Two couples are facing each other. The couples in the middle of
   the set join inside hands (man's right and lady's left) and make an arch.
   The couple on the outside dives under, each couple walks forward. The
   couple making the arch will then do the California twirl while the inside
   couple becomes the active couple and waits for the next call. Count four.

14

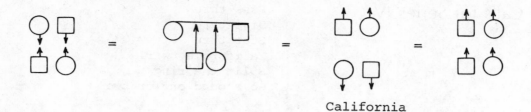

California

STAR THRU: Called to two dancers facing each other. The call is executed
with the man's right and lady's left hand. The man walks forward and
makes a quarter turn to the right while the lady turns counterclockwise
a quarter under the man's raised right arm. The two people end up side-
by-side as partners and remain that way until the next directional call.
Count four.

SPLIT THE RING: The active couple moves forward to the opposite couple and
goes between them. Both the man and the lady go between the couple or the
imaginary ring. Count four.

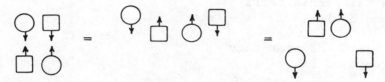

SEPARATE AND GO AROUND ONE OR TWO: This call *follows a pass thru* and *split
the ring*. The two people separate from their partner, man goes to the
left and lady to the right. The two then go around one or two people
depending on the call. When the couple go around two, this returns them to
where they started. Around one person will bring the people between the
inactive couple.

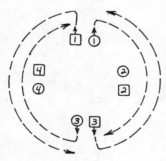

Around Two

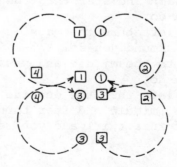

Around One
(Side couples step to side one
step, allowing heads to pass by,
then step back beside partner
after they have passed)

Patter Calls for Series IV

Pass thru
Dive thru
Star thru
California twirl
Split the ring
Go around one or two

REVIEW PREVIOUS CALLS AND KEEP BUILDING WITH THE NEW ONES

Head couples go forward
Star thru-star-thru
Star thru-star-thru
Back up and you're home again.

Head couples go forward
Star thru-then pass thru
Do a do-sa-do
Then right and left thru
Dive to the middle and star thru
Back up and you're home again.

Heads go forward and back
Forward again with a do-sa-do
Then star thru-star thru
Pass thru and do a California twirl
And you're back home again.

Head couples go forward and star thru
Star thru-star thru-pass thru
Do a do-sa-do
Right and left thru the outside two
Dive to the middle and star thru
Pass thru and do a California twirl,
Guess what, you're back home again.

Head couples go forward and back
Forward again and star thru-then pass thru
Do a do-sa-do
Right and left thru the outside two
Turn them around you do
Then dive to the middle and pass thru
Do a do-sa-do
Right and left thru the outside two
Dive to the middle and star thru then pass thru
Do a California twirl and you're back home again.

Separate
(around one)
(around two)

Head couples pass thru, separate go around two.
Do-sa-do your partner. Allemande left corner
    and do a grand right and left.
Meet your partner and promenade her home.

Head couples pass thru and go around two
Back home and everyone swing your partner.
Allemande left your corner and promenade partner.

Head couples pass thru and separate go around one
Into the middle and pass thru, do-sa-do with the outside two.
Right and left thru with the outside two.
Dive thru and star thru--back up, you're home.

Heads pass thru separate and go around one.
Into the middle and do a right and left thru
Pass thru and do-sa-do the outside two.
That's your corner--do an allemande left
Right to your partner for a right and left grand.
Meet your partner and promenade her home.

Head couples pass thru and go around two people.
Down the middle and do a right and left thru.
Pass thru and go around one person--into the middle
    and pass thru. Do-sa-do with the outside two.
Right and left thru, dive thru, star thru
Pass thru separate and go around one person
Into the middle and star thru.
Back up--you're home.

Head couple go forward and pass thru, separate and go
    around one
Into the middle and pass thru
Split the outside two, separate and go around one
Down the middle and star thru, pass thru
Allemande left with the corner and promenade partner home.

Head couples pass thru, separate and go around one
Into the middle and pass thru, split the ring and
    go around one,down the middle and pass thru
Separate and go around one, into the middle and pass thru
Split the ring and go around one and back home again.

Head couples go forward and star thru
Pass thru and do a do-sa-do
Right and left thru the outside two
Dive thru and star thru
Pass thru--separate and go around two
And you're all back home again.

Head couples go forward and back
Forward again and star thru
With the same girl do a California twirl
Then split the ring and go around one
Down the middle for a right and left thru
Pass thru, separate and go around one
Into the middle and star thru
All back home again when you back out from the ring.

Recommended Singing Calls for Series IV

Dime a Dozen
    Blue Star: Number 1676

Everybody Loves a Lover
    MacGregor: Number 8925

Gentle on My Mind
    Wagon Wheel: Number 113

Jambalaya
    Top: Number 25032

Proud Mary
    Kalox: Number K-1116

Winchester Cathedral
    Grenn: Number 12088

CALLS INCLUDED IN SERIES V

Circle to a line
Bend the line
Wheel around
Crosstrail

Series V

CIRCLE TO A LINE: The head or side couple lead to the right; couple one
   leads to two and three goes to four for the heads. For the sides, couple
   two goes to three and four goes to one. The four circle and go three-
   quarters, then the head or side gent breaks out into a line of four. Result
   is that the circle breaks into a line and ends up with two lines facing
   each other with couples one and four diagonally across from each other on
   the left end of the line. When the heads are active, the lines are formed
   where the side couples usually stand.
   Styling: The lady on the end of the line should be turned under the man's
   raised right arm so she is ready when the line is ready.

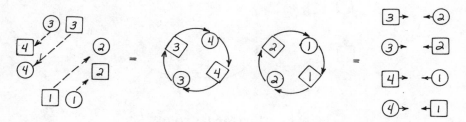

BEND THE LINE: A line with even number of dancers (usually four) breaks in
   the middle. The two in the center back out and the ends of the line
   walk forward a quarter. The result is that the two couples facing out end
   up facing each other after they bend the line.
   Two key points: Prior to bending the line, join inside hands with your
   partner and also keep track of the line of four.

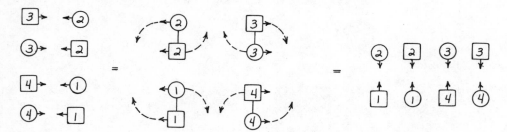

Pass Thru--Bend the Line

19

WHEEL AROUND: From promenade position the couples indicated reverse the line
    of direction and end up with a couple facing a couple in two lines of four.
    The couples wheel by the men backing up and the ladies walking forward.
    The man originally on the inside will now be on the outside of the square.
    The couples wheel in a counterclockwise direction. Count four.

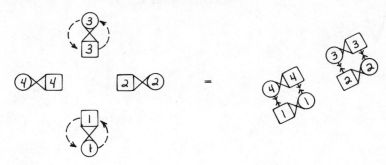

Couples 1 and 3
Wheel Around

CROSSTRAIL: Two active couples start by facing each other. The two couples
    then pass thru, then the lady crosses in front of the man going to the
    left while the man crosses behind the lady and goes to the right.
    The couples then follow the next directional call.
    Pass thru is part of the crosstrail, and it is not called as a separate
    call.

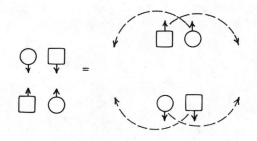

Pass Thru and Cross

20

Patter Calls for Series V

Circle to a line
Bend the line
Wheel around
Crosstrail

Head couples go forward and back
Forward again with a right and left thru
Then crosstrail to the corner
Allemande left the corner
Do-sa-do partner and square your sets.

Head couples go forward and star thru
Pass thru and do a do-sa-do
Right and left thru with the outside two
Dive thru and star thru
Pass thru and separate go around one
    into the middle and star thru
Crosstrail to the corner and do an
    allemande left
Right to partner for a right and left grand

Heads go forward and star thru
With the same girl do a California twirl
Then split the sides and go around one
Down the middle for a right and left thru
Then crosstrail to the corner
Do the old left allemande and grand ole right and left
Promenade eight when you come straight.

Join hands and circle to the left
Then allemande that corner and promenade partner
First and third wheel around and do a right and left thru
Then crosstrail to the corner
Left allemande and a right to partner for a right and left grand
Do-sa-do when you meet partner and promenade home.

Head couples pass thru and go around two
All back home and circle up eight
Allemande left the corner and promenade partner
One and three wheel around and go forward up and back
Pass thru and bend the line
Then do a right and left thru
Pass thru and bend the line
    go forward up and back
Then crosstrail to the corner and do an allemande left
Right to partner for a grand right and left.
Promenade eight when you come straight.

Head couples lead to the right and circle to a line.
Head men break and make a line--forward up and back.
Do a right and left thru and a right and left back
All eight circle to the left--allemande left
Promenade partner.

Head couples lead to the right and circle to a line
Head men break and make a line--forward up and back
Pass thru and bend the line--do a right and left thru.
Go forward and back and pass thru
Bend the line and do a right and left thru.
All eight circle to the left--do an allemande left
Give a right to your partner and do a right and left grand.
Meet your partner and promenade home.

Head couples do a star thru and pass thru.
Do-sa-do with the outside two--star thru.
Pass thru and bend the line--forward up and back.
Do a right and left thru--pass thru and bend the line.
Star thru and do a right and left thru
Dive thru and star thru--back up, you're home.

Head couples pass thru and go around one person.
Into the middle and pass thru--do-sa-do with the outside two
Star thru and pass thru and bend the line
Star thru, star thru-pass thru and bend the line
Forward up and back--star thru--right and left thru
Dive thru--pass thru and do an allemande left with corner
Right to your partner and do a right and left grand.
Meet your partner and promenade.

Recommended Singing Calls for Series V

Amapola
    Top: Number 25030

April Showers
    Blue Star Record: Number 1604

Five Foot Two
    Square Your Sets: Number 1001

Goodbye Lady Love
    Top: Number 25096

Tipperary
    Balance: Number X110

CALLS INCLUDED IN SERIES VI

Substitute
Box the gnat
Box the flea
Pull-by

Series VI

SUBSTITUTE: Two couples facing in the same direction with one couple in
   front of the other couples. The couple in front makes an arch by joining
   inside hands (man's right and lady's left) and backs over the couple
   behind them. The result is that the two couples have exchanged places.

BOX THE GNAT: Two people facing each other join right hands. The lady
   moves under the man's raised right arm by moving counterclockwise. The
   man walks forward and makes a half turn to his right. The result is that
   the two people merely exchange places and they end facing each other. Count
   four.

BOX THE FLEA: Two people facing each other join left hands. The lady moves
   under the man's raised left arm by moving clockwise. The man walks forward and makes a half turn to his left. The result is that the two people
   merely exchange places and end facing each other. Count four.

PULL-BY: This call follows box the gnat and box the flea. The two people merely pull-by on the same side that hands are joined.

Right   Left

Patter Calls for Series VI

Circle to the left-face corner and do an allemande left
Box the gnat with partner--pull-by--box the flea with corner
Pull-by and do a right and left grand
Meet partner and promenade her home.

Allemande left with the corner
Give a right to partner and do a right and left grand
Meet your partner and do box the gnat
Pull-by, allemande left with the corner
Promenade partner.

Head couples go forward and box the gnat
Pull-by separate and go around one person
Into the middle and box the gnat--pull-by
Allemande left with the corner and promenade partner.

Head couples pass thru separate and go around one person
Into the middle and box the gnat--pull-by
Split the outside two and go around one person
Down the middle and pass thru
Separate and go around one person
Into the middle and star thru
Back out, you're home again.

Allemande left with the corner--box the gnat with partner
Pull-by and box the flea with corner--pull-by
Do-sa-do with partner and the men star left
Box the gnat with partner--pull-by
Allemande left with the corner and promenade partner home.

Men star left and when you meet partner star promenade
Ladies backtrack and box the gnat with partner
Pull-by allemande left with the corner
Give a right to partner and do a right and left grand
Meet partner and box the gnat--pull-by
Allemande left with the corner
Back to partner and promenade home.

Head couples star thru and substitute
New centers star thru and star thru and substitute
New centers star thru, star thru and substitute
New centers star thru, star thru and substitute
New center star thru, back out, you're home again.

Practice Calls for Series VI

Head couples star thru, pass thru and do-sa-do with the outside two
Right and left thru, dive thru and substitute
Pass thru and do-sa-do, right and left thru
Dive thru and pass thru and do-sa-do
Right and left thru and dive thru,
Substitute, star thru, back up, you're home.

Head couples star thru, pass thru and do-sa-do
Right and left thru and dive thru
Substitute, substitute, star thru
Back up, you're home.

Head couples pass thru separate and go around one
Into the middle and substitute
Pass thru and do-sa-do with the outside two
Right and left thru, dive thru
Pass thru and do-sa-do
Right and left thru, dive thru and substitute
Pass thru, right and left thru
Dive thru, star thru, back up, you're home.

Recommended Singing Calls for Series VI

It's Later Than You Think
   Keeno: Number 2150

Let's Go Back to Donegal
   Top: Number 25036

Little Arrows
   Top: Number 25186

MaryAnn
   Windsor: Number 4815

Ragtime Piano
   Windsor: Number 4803

There'll Be Some Changes Made
   Blue Star: Number 1631

Yes Sir
   Old Timer: Number 8177

You've Gotta Be Puttin Me On
   Grenn: Number 12101

Grand square
Square thru
    A. full
    B. half
    C. three-quarter

Series VII

GRAND SQUARE: A simultaneous movement wherein the sides are doing one movement and the heads are doing another. The action for the heads is to move
forward four steps, turn a quarter turn to face partner, and back away
four steps, turn a quarter turn to face opposite and back away four steps,
turn a quarter turn to face partner, and walk forward four steps. Count:
sixteen.
The sides start by facing partner and backing up four steps, turn and
quarter turn and face opposite and walk forward four, turn to face partner and walk forward four, turn to face partner and back up four steps.
Count: sixteen steps.

From this point the action is reversed. In other words, the heads will
do the sides part and the sides will be doing the head parts.

Note: Tell the dancers to never turn their backs on anyone.

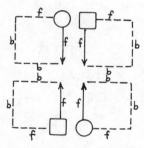

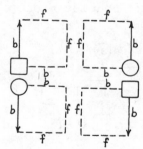

Heads: forward--back--back--forward   Sides: back--forward--forward--back

SQUARE THRU
    A. Full Square Thru: Executed with two facing couples. Take opposite's
       right hand, pull on by, turn a quarter turn to face partner; take
       partner's left hand, pull on by, turn and take opposite's right hand,
       pull on by, turn and take partner's left hand, pull on by.

Note: Right, pull-by, turn; left, pull-by, and turn, right, pull-by turn left, pull-by but you do not turn.
In a full square thru--end up facing your corner.

B. Half Square Thru: Executed with two facing couples. The one-half square thru is just two hands. Couples go forward giving a right hand to their opposite, pull-by and turn, giving a left hand to their partner, pulling by, but do not turn.

Note: In a one-half square thru end up facing your right hand girl.

C. Three-quarter Square Thru: Executed with two facing couples. The three-quarter thru is just three hands. Couples go forward giving right hand to their opposite, pull-by and turn, giving a left hand to their partner, pull-by and turn, giving a right hand to their opposite, pull-by, but do not turn.

Note: The couples end up in their home position facing out.

28

Patter Calls for Series VII

Square thru
A. full
B. half
C. three-quarter

REVIEW THE PREVIOUS CALLS AND KEEP BUILDING WITH THE NEW ONES.

Head couples go forward and back
Forward again with a full square thru
Corner do-sa-do
Right and left thru, turn the girls
Dive to the middle and star thru
Crosstrail to the corner--left allemande
Square your sets.

Head couple go forward and do a full square thru
Corner do-sa-do
Right and left thru then dive to the middle
Pass thru--do a do-sa-do.
Right and left thru--turn the girls
Dive thru and pass thru
Guess who--corner-left allemande
Do-sa-do your partner and square your sets.

Head couple do a full square thru
Then do a right and left thru
Dive to the middle and pass thru
Right and left thru and turn the girls
Dive to the middle and star thru
Pass thru--separate around just one and
    into the middle and star thru
Crosstrail to the corner--left allemande
Do-sa-do partner and square your sets.

Head couples do a full square thru
Do-sa-do the corner and do a left allemande
Then right to your partner for a right and left grand
Promenade eight when you come straight.

Head couple do a three-quarter square thru
Separate and go around two
Then crosstrail to the corner--left allemande
Do-sa-do partner and square your sets.

Head couple do a three-quarter square thru
Separate and go around one into the middle and
    pass thru--there's the corner--left allemande
And a grand old right and left.
Promenade eight when you come straight.

One and three go up and back, square thru
Four hand around and do a right and left thru
Dive back thru, square thru, three-quarters round
Left allemande go home and do a do-sa-do
Then square your sets.

Allemande left your corner and promenade partner
Heads wheel around and do a star thru
Then square thru, three-quarters round
Find the corner left allemande and do
    a grand old right and left.
Promenade eight when you come straight.

Head couples promenade halfway round
Then do a right and left thru--turn your girl
Then the four ladies do a grand chain
The sides do a full square thru--go four hands
Find the corner and do a do-sa-do
Then left allemande and a grand old right and left
Meet your partner and promenade eight.

Heads do a full square thru--go four hands
Corner do-sa-do--once around
Pass thru--find a new corner and do a left allemande
Go back to your old corner and promenade the set.

One and three go up and back and then do a right and left thru
Then star thru and pass thru and right and left thru again
Dive to the middle and square thru--three-quarters around
And then find the corner--left allemande
Do-sa-do your partner and square your sets.

Head couples do a full square thru
Then do a three-quarter square thru with the outside two
Heads do a half square thru and
    a California twirl and you're back home again.

Circle to the left--face the corner and do an allemande left
Box the gnat with partner--pull-by--box the flea with corner
Pull-by and do a right and left grand.

Allemande left with the corner
Give a right to your partner and do a right and left grand.
Meet your partner and do box the gnat
Pull-by, allemande left with the corner
Promenade partner.

Head couples go forward and do box the gnat
Pull-by separate and go around one person
Into the middle and box the gnat--pull-by
Allemande left with corner and promenade partner.

Head couples pass thru separate and go around one person
Into the middle and box the gnat--pull-by
Split the outside two and go around one person
Down the middle and pass thru separate and go around one person
Into the middle and star thru
Back up, you're home again.

Allemande left with the corner--box the gnat with partner
Pull-by and box the flea with the corner--pull-by
Do-sa-do with partner and the men star left
Box the gnat with partner, pull-by
Allemande left with corner and promenade partner.

Men star left and when you meet your partner
Star promenade.
Ladies backtrack and box the gnat with partner
Pull-by, allemande left with the corner
Give a right to your partner and do a right and left grand.
Meet your partner--box the gnat--pull-by
Allemande left with corner and promenade partner.

Recommended Singing Calls for Series VII

Are You From Dixie
   Sets In Order: Number 124

Chewing Gum
   Go Records: Number 104

Grand Square
   Sets In Order: Number F102

June Night
   Sets In Order: Number 127

Lady Be Good
   Grenn: Number 12043

Ragtime Banjo Ball
   Top: Number 25035

The Possum Song
   Blue Star: Number 1630

Thunder Road
   Windsor: Number 4809

Wheels Q
   Top: Number 25075

When You're Swinging
   Lore: Number 1017

Tick-A-Tack
   MacGregor: Number 1070

CALLS INCLUDED IN SERIES VIII

Wheel and deal
Double pass thru
Cloverleaf

Series VIII

WHEEL AND DEAL: Called from a line of four dancers facing out. The right
hand couple of the line wheels left and the left hand couple wheels right.
The left hand couple ends up behind the right hand couple. The wheel is
done in promenade position. Easy way to remember which is left and right
hand couple of the line--the man closest to the center of the line of four
is the right hand couple and should be in front.

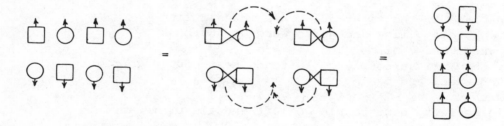

DOUBLE PASS THRU: Two sets of couples facing each other start by passing
right shoulders. The couples pass both couples and end up facing away
from the center. The call that usually follows this is the first couple
go left and the next couple go right resulting in the couples ending in
a line facing each other.

CLOVERLEAF: This call follows a double pass thru. The couples separate from their partners and each line walking forward and making a leaf of the four-leaf clover. Result is that they move into another double pass thru formation with a new partner. The people behind must stay behind--like follow the leader.

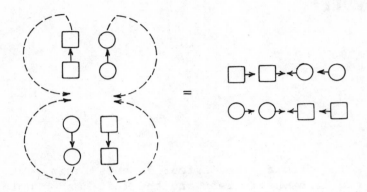

Patter Calls for Series VIII

Head couples lead to the right and break makes a line
Head men break into a line and go forward up and back
Pass thru, wheel and deal
Double pass thru, first couple go left and next couple go right
Pass thru and wheel and deal
Double pass thru
First couple go left, next couple go left and all promenade.

Head couples lead to the right and make a line
Go forward up and back
Pass thru, wheel and deal
Double pass thru, first couple go left and second couple go right
Right and left thru, star thru
Pass thru, allemande left with the corner
Give a right to partner for a right and left grand
Meet partner and promenade home.

Head couples lead to the right and make a line
Forward up and back, pass thru
Wheel and deal and substitute
Double pass thru, first couple go right and second couple left
Do a right and left thru, star thru
Pass thru, allemande left with the corner
Promenade partner.

34

Head couples lead to the right and make a line
Forward up and back, pass thru, wheel and deal
Double pass thru, first go left and second go right
Do a right and left thru, pass thru
Wheel and deal, double pass thru
First couple go left and second go right
Star thru, pass thru, allemande left with the corner
Give a right to partner for a right and left grand
Meet partner and promenade her home.

Head couples promenade halfway around the set and chain the ladies
Heads lead out to the right and circle to a line
Go forward up and back
Pass thru and wheel and deal
Double pass thru and cloverleaf
Centers star thru and back out
Everyone's home again.

Practice Calls for Series VIII

Head couples lead to the right and make a line
Head men break into a line go forward up and back
Pass thru, wheel and deal
Double pass thru, first couple go left and
    the second couple go left.
All promenade.

Head couples lead to the right and make a line
Forward up and back
Pass thru and wheel and deal
Double pass thru, first couple go left and
    second couple go right
Right and left thru, star thru
Pass thru, allemande left with the corner
Give a right to your partner and do a
    right and left grand.
Meet your partner and promenade.

Head couples lead to the right and make a line
Forward up and back, pass thru
Wheel and deal and substitute
Double pass thru, first couple go right and
    the second couple go left
Do a right and left thru, star thru
Pass thru, allemande left with the corner
Promenade partner.

Head couples lead to the right and make a line
Forward up and back, pass thru, wheel and deal
Double pass thru, first go left and the second go right
Do a right and left thru, pass thru
Wheel and deal, double pass thru
First couple go left and the second couple go right
Star thru, pass thru, allemande left with corner
Give a right to your partner and do a right
    and left grand.
Meet partner and promenade her home.

Head couples star thru and pass thru
Circle up four with the outside two
Break out into a line, head men break
Go forward up and back, pass thru
Wheel and deal, centers star thru, pass thru and
    cloverleaf
New centers square thru, three-quarters
Allemande left with the corner and promenade partner.

Head couples lead to the right and circle to a line
Head men break into a line forward up and back
Pass thru, wheel and deal, double pass thru
First couple go left and second go right
Pass thru and bend the line, go forward up and back
Right and left thru, pass thru and bend the line
Pass thru, wheel and deal, double pass thru
First couple go left and next go right
Star thru, pass thru, allemande left with the corner
    and right to partner for a grand right and left
Promenade eight when you come straight.

Recommended Singing Calls for Series VIII

Big Daddy
   Grenn: Number 12035

Old Black Magic
   Hi-Hat: Number 330

Give My Regards to Broadway
   Blue Star: Number 1623

Ride, Ride, Ride
   Grenn: Number 12093

King of the Road
   Wagon Wheel: Number 109

Swinging Billy Joe
   Wagon Wheel: Number 108

Mister Piano Man
   MacGregor: Number 1061

Summer Sounds
   MacGregor: Number 2051

Styling Techniques for Beginning Series

The pleasure of square dance comes not only from performing the skills, but also from styling those skills, giving the calls, sets, and dancers a touch of class, beauty, and smoothness. The following suggestions can help your group style their sets for that something extra.

1. GENTS: When standing in the set between calls or as an inactive couple the gentleman should always hold the lady's hand in his. The gent's hand is underneath, while the lady's hand lies on top. Both hands are about waist height.

2. LADIES: When performing calls such as: Do-sa-do, See-Saw, and Weave the Ring; the lady should hold onto her skirt with both hands--flaring it outward slightly. When performing calls such as: Allemande Left, Ladies Chain, and Ladies Star the lady should hold her skirt with her free hand--flaring it outward slightly.
The gent on the other hand when performing calls such as Do-sa-do, See-Saw, and Weave the Ring should place his hands behind his back in a clasped position or place them near his hip pockets. All other times the gentleman's hands are at his side or used to perform calls.

3. BUZZ SWING FLOURISH: From the closed dance position of the buzz swing the man starts the flourish with his left hand, which is holding the lady's right hand, by starting the lady in a clockwise turn at his side. Immediately after starting the lady in her turn he raises his left arm upward with the lady's right hand in contact. The dancers' arms form an archway for the lady to complete her turn under. After the lady finishes her turn, both dancers drop hands and face to the center of the set, and wait for the next directional call. When a promenade is the next call, the gent maintains hand contact with the lady's right hand throughout the turn. When the turn is completed the gent lowers his left hand in front of the couple and places the lady's right hand in his, and they regrasp left hands under their right (promenade hand position) and proceed forward in line of direction of the promenade.

4. PROMENADE FLOURISH: Upon the last step returning home from the promenade, the couple lifts both arms upward above their heads. When both arms are raised, they release left hands, maintaining contact with the right hand, and the lady walks forward in a clockwise circle turn. A small archway is formed by the dancers' right arms, under which the lady completes her turn. After the turn is completed, the dancers drop hands and face toward the center of the set and proceed with the next directional call.

5. GRAND RIGHT AND LEFT FLOURISH: As you meet your partner on the last hand (right) contact of the grand right and left and a promenade is the next directional call, the gent pulls the lady towards him raising both dancers' right hands and forms an archway. The lady then makes a half counterclockwise turn under the raised archway. After the turn is completed, the couple lower their right arms and rejoin left hands under the right (promenade hand position) and proceed in line of direction of the promenade.

6. DO-SA-DO HALF TURNS: When performing the do-sa-do from a circle or square formation and between a partner and his corner the dancers can perform the do-sa-do flourish. The dancers, facing one another, pass right shoulders. Immediately after passing right shoulders, both dancers pivot a half turn to the left and face each other again. They then pass right shoulders again back to their starting position and face to the center of the set or the next directional call.

7. SEE-SAW HALF TURNS: The see-saw half turn is the same as the do-sa-do half turn, with the exceptions of: the first passing of shoulders is left instead of right, the half pivot is to the right, and the second passing of shoulders is with the left again.

Note: Many times the do-sa-do and see-saw half turns will put the dancers in a better position to execute the next call with their partner or to proceed with the next directional call in the set.

Series IX

PAIR OFF: The couples are in set formation. The couples indicated walk toward the center of the set and turn to face their corner.

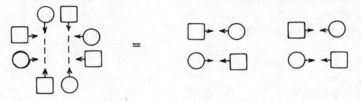

OCEAN WAVE: Usually follows a do-sa-do all the way around the corner and
into an ocean wave. Formed from one couple facing another couple. The
people facing walk up to each other, right shoulder to right shoulder,
ending up facing in alternate directions. The wave rocks forward and back-
ward two steps. The hands are in a hands up position to each other.

Rock Forward   Wave   Rock Back

SWING THRU: Performed from a line of four dancers, ocean wave position. The
line breaks in the middle and the people turn halfway around in a right
hand turn. Then the two in the center turn halfway around with a left hand
turn. The hands are in a hands up position. Cue words: right halfway and
left in the middle.

BOYS TRADE--GIRLS TRADE: In a line of four, ocean wave position, the boys or
    girls trade places by walking forward. The dancers stay in the same ocean
    wave position.

Boys Trade   Girls Trade

Patter Calls for Series IX

Head couples go forward and back
Into the middle and pair off
Do-sa-do, all the way around into
    an ocean wave
Rock the wave forward and back
Swing thru, swing thru
Boys trade, girls trade and do
    a right and left thru
Dive thru and square thru three hands
Allemande left the corner and promenade partner home.

Head couples go forward and pair off
Do-sa-do, all the way around and make a wave
Rock the wave forward and back and do a
    right and left thru.
Dive thru, pass thru, do-sa-do
    all the way around into an ocean wave
Right and left thru, dive thru
Star thru, back up, you're home.

Head couples go forward and pair off
Do-sa-do with the outside two
All the way around into an ocean wave
Rock the wave--swing thru
Boys trade and box the gnat
Right and left thru, dive thru
Star thru, crosstrail to the corner
Allemande left, right to partner for a
    grand right and left.
Meet partner and promenade home.

Head couples go forward and pair off
Do-sa-do with the outside two
All the way around into an ocean wave
Rock the wave and do a right and left thru
Dive thru, pass thru, do a do-sa-do
All the way around into an ocean wave
Swing thru, swing thru again
Right and left thru, dive thru
Substitute, star thru
Back up, you're home.

Head couples go forward and do a do-sa-do
All the way around into an ocean wave
Rock forward and back and do a right and left thru
Pass thru, separate and go around one
Into the middle and pass thru
Do-sa-do the outside two
All the way around into an ocean wave
Swing thru, boys trade, box the gnat
Right and left thru, dive thru
Square thru three hands
Allemande left with the corner
Right to partner for a right and left grand
Meet partner and promenade her home.

Head couples square thru four hands
Do-sa-do the outside two
All the way around into an ocean wave
Rock the wave forward and back
Swing thru, swing thru
Boys trade, girls trade and
    do a right and left thru
Dive thru, pass thru
Right and left thru the outside two
Dive thru, star thru, back up, you're home.

Head couples pair off and do-sa-do
All the way around into an ocean wave
Swing thru, boys trade, girls trade
Swing thru, right and left thru
Dive thru, square thru three hands
Allemande left the corner and promenade partner.

Recommended Singing Calls for Series IX

Everything is Rosy Now
 Lore: Number 1019

Full Time Job
 MacGregor: Number 1001

Just in Time
 Hi-Hat: Number 254

Saturday Night
 Jay-Bar: Number L5006

Six Days on the Road
 Began: Number 1160

That's Where My Baby Used to Be
 Blue Star: Number 1820

Whispering
 Balance: Number 403

Wildflower
 Scope: Number 512

You Do Something to Me
 Aqua: Number 113

CALLS INCLUDED IN SERIES X

Turn thru
Double swing thru
Alamo style balance

Series X

TURN THRU: This is an allemande right in a hands up position. The dancers move around each other and wait for the next directional call.

DOUBLE SWING THRU: The dancers are in an ocean wave position and execute two swing thrus. Dancers turn right halfway, left in the middle, then right halfway and left in the middle.

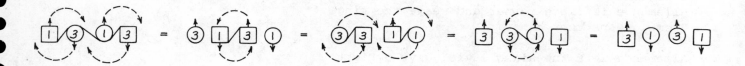

ALAMO STYLE BALANCE: Dancers are in square formation and then give their left hands to the corner as if executing an allemande left, only in hands up position. The dancers end up in a circle alternately facing in or out with hands joined. The dancers rock forward and back two steps.
Cue words: Allemande left the alamo style, and balance forward and back.

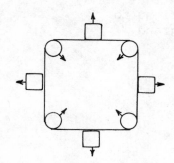

Patter Calls for Series X

Head couples do a right and left thru
Side ladies chain
Sides square thru--count four hands
With the heads do-sa-do, all the way around
    to an ocean wave
Swing thru, then turn thru and
    allemande left corner
Promenade partner home.

Heads promenade halfway around
Lead right and circle four
Head men break into a line--forward and back
Star thru across from you
Do-sa-do--full around to an ocean wave
Swing thru, boys trade
Box the gnat and then pull-by
Allemande left the corner and promenade.

Heads lead right--you circle to a line
Do a right and left thru
Pass thru--wheel and deal--then substitute
Center four swing thru--then turn thru
Allemande left the corner--grand ole right and left
Promenade eight when you come straight.

Heads promenade halfway round
Down the middle, swing thru, turn thru
Separate and go around one, into the center
Swing thru and then turn thru
Allemande left the corner and weave the ring.
Promenade partner home.

Allemande left the alamo style, give a right
    to partner and balance away.
Turn thru with partner, allemande left corner
Promenade partner home.

Allemande left the alamo style, give a right to
    partner and balance away
Swing thru and balance once again
Swing thru and then turn thru
Allemande left with the corner, right to
    partner for a right and left grand
Promenade partner home.

Allemande left the alamo style, give a right
    to partner and balance away
Swing thru, balance, swing thru
Box the gnat with partner, pull-by
Allemande left corner, do-sa-do partner
    and promenade her home.

Allemande left the alamo style, give a right
    to partner and balance,
Double swing thru, turn thru
Allemande left with the corner
Grand ole right and left, promenade home.

Heads go forward and back, pair off
Do-sa-do go full around
Ocean wave and rock forward and back
Double swing thru, boys trade, girls trade
Right and left thru, dive thru
Pass thru, do-sa-do go full around
Make ocean wave, rock forward and back
Double swing thru, boys trade, girls trade
Right and left thru, dive thru
Star thru, back out, you're home.

Recommended Singing Calls for Series X

Baby That's Living
    Hi-Hat: Number 361

Baby Won't You Please Come Home
    Kalox: Number LH 169

Down in Dixie
    Longhorn: Number LH 170A

My Window Faces the South
    Kalox: Number B115

The Greatest
    Windsor: Number 4955

Yes Yes
    Windsor: Number 4890

Series XI

SLIDE THRU: This is a star thru without hands. Dancers start by facing
each other. The man walks forward and makes a quarter turn to the
right while the girl makes a quarter turn to the left (counterclockwise)
in front of the man. The result is that the two dancers end up side by
side as partners.

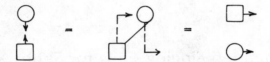

PARTNER TRADE: This is a California twirl without hands. Dancers start facing
out and side by side. The man walks around in front of the lady and ends
facing back toward the center. The lady turns around counterclockwise and
ends up facing back toward the center of the set.

TRADE BY: The dancers are in a position where the center four are facing
inward and the end four are facing outward. Those facing inward pass thru
while those facing outward do a partner trade.

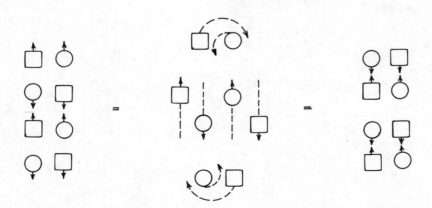

46

Patter Calls for Series XI

Head couples pair off--do-sa-do full around
Make an ocean wave and rock forward and back
Swing thru--swing thru
Boys trade
Girls trade
Slide thru--pass thru--wheel and deal
Double pass thru--first couple go left and
    next couple go right
Slide thru--right and left thru
Dive thru and substitute
Square thru--three hands
Allemande left the corner and promenade partner.

Head couples forward and slide thru
Pass thru and do a do-sa-do full around
Make an ocean wave and rock
Swing thru--swing thru
Boys trade
Girls trade
Slide thru--pass thru
Bend the line--forward up and back
Right and left thru--pass thru
Bend the line--slide thru
Right and left thru
Dive thru--star thru, back out, you're home.

Head couples pair off--do-sa-do full around
Make an ocean wave, rock forward and back
Swing thru--swing thru
Boys trade
Girls trade
Slide thru--pass thru--partner trade
Forward up and back--slide thru
Right and left thru--dive thru
Square thru three hands--allemande left corner
Right to partner for a right and left grand
Meet partner and promenade home.

Head couples slide thru--pass thru
Do-sa-do full around
Make an ocean wave and rock
Swing thru--swing thru
Boys trade--girls trade
Slide thru--pass thru--partner trade
Pass thru--wheel and deal
Double pass thru--first couple go left and
    next couple go right
Slide thru--right and left thru
Dive thru--star thru
Back out, you're home.

Heads pair off--pass thru
Trade by and do-sa-do the outside two
Full around--ocean wave
Swing thru--boys trade
Box the gnat--right and left thru
Dive thru--pass thru
Do-sa-do outside two
Full around to an ocean wave
Swing thru--swing thru
Boys trade--girls trade
Right and left thru
Dive thru--substitute
Star thru--pass thru--partner trade
Back out, home again.

Recommended Singing Calls for Series XI

Snowbird
   Hi-Hat: Number 397

Under the Sun
   Top: Number 325276

Wave Goodbye to Me
   MacGregor: Number 2035

CALLS INCLUDED IN SERIES XII

Men run
Circulate men
Circulate ladies
All eight circulate
Couples circulate

Series XII

MEN RUN: From an ocean wave with the men in the middle, the man moves around
behind the girl on his right. The dancers end in couple formation with
one couple facing in and one couple facing out.

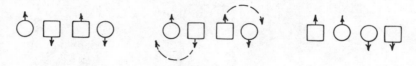

MEN CIRCULATE: All the men are facing in a certain direction in ocean wave
formation. The men move forward one-quarter, taking the next person's
place.

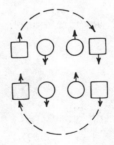

LADIES CIRCULATE: All the ladies are facing in a certain direction in an
ocean wave formation. The ladies move one-quarter, taking the next lady's
place.

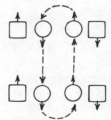

49

ALL EIGHT CIRCULATE: The dancers are in two ocean wave formations. All
    dancers move one position, ending in two ocean waves.

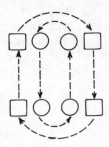

COUPLES CIRCULATE: The dancers are in an ocean wave position. The call
    men run right will put the couples in position to circulate. The couples
    move one position forward in a counterclockwise direction.

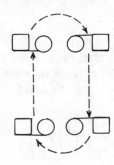

Patter Calls for Series XII

Heads right and left thru--sides do the same,
Heads square thru--four hands
Do-sa-do the corner
Make an ocean wave--balance
All eight circulate
Star thru and right and left thru
Star thru and allemande left, swing your partner.

Four ladies chain three-quarters round
Heads square thru--four hands
Then swing thru--boys run
Couples circulate
Wheel and deal and face these two
Pass thru and allemande left

Four ladies chain
Couples one-three square thru--four hands
Do-sa-do--make a wave
Just the men circulate--rock
Change hands--allemande left--promenade.

Heads square thru--four hands
Swing thru
Boys trade--girls circulate
Turn thru--go left allemande.

Head couples go forward and back
Heads pair off--do-sa-do full around
Make an ocean wave--rock forward and back
Swing thru--men run right
Wheel and deal--right and left thru
Dive thru and square thru three hands
Allemande left corner and promenade partner.

Head couples pair off--do-sa-do full around
Makes an ocean wave and rock
Swing thru, men run right
Wheel and deal--right and left thru
Dive thru--pass thru
Do-sa-do--go full around
Make an ocean wave and rock
Swing thru--men run right
Wheel and deal--right and left thru
Dive thru--star thru--back out, you're home.

Head couples pair off--do-sa-do full around
Make an ocean wave--rock forward and back
Swing thru--men run right
Couples circulate--two places
Wheel and deal--right and left thru
Dive thru and substitute
Pass thru--do-sa-do outside two
Right and left thru--dive thru--substitute
Star thru--back out, you're home.

Recommended Singing Calls for Series XII

No More No Less
    Hi-Hat: Number 334

Pass Me By
    MacGregor: Number 1064

Ring of Fire
    Jay Bar Kay: Number 118

CALLS INCLUDED IN SERIES XIII

Allemande thar star
Wrong way thar star
Shoot the star
Slip the clutch
Throw in the clutch

Series XIII

ALLEMANDE THAR STAR: Dancers form a right hand star by moving in with a left
   hand turn. Men turn ladies by a left hand turn and move in and make a right
   hand star. The ladies are on their free arms facing in opposite direction.
   The men back up and the ladies walk forward.

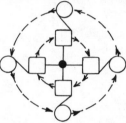

WRONG WAY THAR STAR: Dancers form a left hand star by moving in with a right
   hand turn. Men turn the ladies by a right hand turn and move into a left
   hand star. The ladies are on the men's free arm facing in the opposite direction. The men back up and the ladies walk forward.

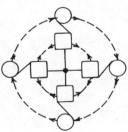

SHOOT THE STAR: This is one method of releasing the allemande thar star or
   the wrong way thar star. The star is released in the middle and the couples
   turn halfway around each other and follow the next directional call.

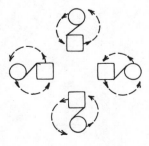

THROW IN THE CLUTCH: This is a second method for releasing the allemande thar star and the wrong way star. Those in the center retain the star but release hand holds with the ladies on the outside. The star then changes directions while those on the outside continue to walk forward. Continue walking in that direction until the next call.

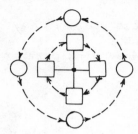

SLIP THE CLUTCH: This is a third method of releasing the allemande thar star and the wrong way thar star. Those in the center stop and release hand hold with the outside person. The men then give that same hand to the next person coming toward them on the outside and follow the next directional call.

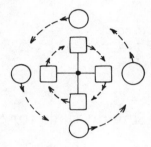

Patter Calls for Series XIII

Allemande left like an allemande thar
Go right and left--gents make a right hand star
Shoot that star, full turn, your corner box the gnat
Pull-by--grand right and left.

Allemande left, allemande thar,
Go right and left and star
The men back up a right hand star
Shoot the star--do-sa-do partner
Allemande left.

Turn your corner by the right and make a wrong way thar
Shoot the star, left and right box the gnat
Do-sa-do right after that (same girl)
Allemande left, grand right and left

Allemande left, allemande thar,
Go right and left and the four gents star
Gents back up, make a right hand star
Now slip the clutch--left allemande--swing partner

Allemande left go allemande thar
Right and left and make a star
Shoot that star go full around
Turn corner right hand round
Partner left hand round and promenade.

Promenade around
All four couples backtrack
Girls turn back and meet the gent
Turn him left you know
A full turn around and slip the clutch
Your corners allemande, promenade partner.

Recommended Singing Calls for Series XIII

Bare Necessities
   Top: Number 25169

Coney Island Washboard Gal
   Grenn: Number 12089

Dixieland Swing
   Flip: Number 117

Don't Want to Be Alone
   Began: Number 1212

Every Little Rose Bud
   Grenn: Number 12106

Exactly Like You
   Top: Number 25029

I Don't Love Nobody
   MacGregor: Number 1027

Kingston Town
   Grenn: Number 12033

Swing That Baby Now
   Blue Star: Number 1563

Texas Plains
   Windsor: Number 4891

You Can't Have My Love
   Lore: Number 1052

Series XIV

SPIN CHAIN THRU: Four couples are arranged in two parallel ocean waves.
Those in the center release hand holds and all four couples turn by the
right halfway around. Then the two in the center of each wave turn by the
left three-quarters around to make an ocean wave across the set. The two
in the center of this wave across the set and turn halfway around by the
right to form the wave across the set once again. Then the wave breaks in
the middle and the two turn by the left three-quarters to finish in two
similar parallel ocean waves.

SPIN THE TOP: From an ocean wave formation, the two in the center break and
turn halfway around by the right. Then the two in the center turn by the
left three-quarters. While the centers are turning three-quarters, the end
dancers move forward one-quarter. The result is that the dancers end in
another ocean wave but the lines are at right angles to the starting line.

Patter Calls for Series XIV

One and three star thru--California twirl
Do-sa-do the outside two
Make an ocean wave
Swing thru two by two
Spin the top
Go right and left thru
Star thru--circle up four
Halfway round--allemande left--promenade partner.

Heads lead right and circle to a line
Do a right and left thru in front of you
Do-sa-do--make an ocean wave
Girls trade--spin the top
When you meet the girl--turn thru
Left allemande--swing partner--promenade.

Head couples pair off--do-sa-do
Full around to an ocean wave
Spin chain thru
Girls double circulate
Turn thru--allemande left corner
Promenade partner home.

Head couples pair off--do-sa-do
Full around to an ocean wave
Spin chain thru
All eight circulate
Turn thru--allemande left corner
Right to partner for a grand right and left
Promenade partner.

Head couples square thru four hands
Do-sa-do the outside two
Full around to an ocean wave
Spin chain thru
Spin chain thru
Swing thru--swing thru
Boys trade
Girls trade
Right and left thru--dive thru
Square thru--three hands
Corners left allemande
Grand ole right and left--promenade.

Head couples pass thru--separate go
   around one person
Into the middle and pass thru
Do-sa-do the outside two--full around
Make an ocean wave and swing thru
Boys trade--box the gnat
Right and left thru
Dive thru
Pass thru--do-sa-do full around
Make an ocean wave and swing thru
Swing thru
Boys trade--girls trade
Spin chain thru
All eight circulate
Turn thru
Allemande left the corner
Promenade partner.

Head couples pair off--do-sa-do
Full around to an ocean wave
Swing thru--spin the top
Slide thru--right and left thru
Dive thru--pass thru
Do-sa-do full around
Ocean wave and rock
Swing thru--spin the top
Slide thru--right and left thru
Dive thru
Star thru--back out, you're home.

Recommended Singing Calls for Series XIV

Help Me Make It Through the Night
   MacGregor: Number 134

Loves to Swing
   Windsor: Number 4892

Long Lonesome Highway
   Wagon Wheel: Number 309

Looking Out My Backdoor
   Red Beet: Number 114

Under Your Spell
   Windsor: Number 4894A

Primrose Lane
   MacGregor: Number 2081

Raindrops Keep Fallin' on My Head
   Jay-Bar-Kay: Number 107

Something Stupid
   Hi-Hat: Number 357

The First Thing Every Morning
   Blue Star: Number 1827

That's a No No
   Windsor: Number 4937

Promenade red hot
Left square thru
Dopaso

Series XV

PROMENADE RED HOT: The dancers are in promenade formation. Red hot is a
series of four forearm turns. The lady in the couple in front turns back
to the man behind and turns by the right forearm. Then partner left, all
the way around one and half times, to the corner right, and then back to
partner left. The couples end back in promenade formation.

LEFT SQUARE THRU: This is the same movement as the square thru except the
dancers start with the left hand. This results with the man turning on
the inside of the lady to the right and the lady turning to the left.

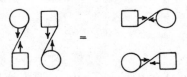

DOPASO: The dancers are in circle formation. Each dancer turns partner with
a left forearm turn. After turning completely around, each dancer gives
right forearm to the corner. Then returning to partner does a courtesy turn
in place. The Dopaso can be done from other positions besides the circle,
but this is the beginning formation.

Patter Calls for Series XV

Allemande left the corner and promenade
Go red hot--right hand lady right; partner left
   all the way around; corner right; partner left
Promenade.

Allemande left the corner--box the gnat with partner
Pull-by--allemande left
Promenade partner
Go red hot
Promenade partner home.

Head couple go forward and back
Do a left square thru
Allemande left the corner
Right to partner for a right and left grand
Meet partner and promenade
Go red hot
Promenade.

Head couples go forward and back
Do a left square thru
Split the outside two--around one
Back home again.

Join hands and circle to the left
Break the circle with a Dopaso
Promenade partner.

Recommended Singing Calls for Series XV

Walking to Kansas City
   Kalox: Number 1028

Walking in the Sunshine
   Wagon Wheel: Number 112

Series XVI

DIXIE CHAIN: The starting formation begins with two couples facing each other
   in a single line formation, with the ladies in front of their partners.
   The dancers move toward each other performing a movement like the right and
   left grand. The ladies join right hands and pull-by; giving left hands to
   the men facing them and pull-by. The two men then join right hands and pull-
   by. The couples end in a single file formation as in the beginning.

DIXIE STYLE: This movement starts like a dixie chain but ends in an ocean
   wave formation. Those in the lead join right hands and pull-by, then left
   hand to the next and pull-by. Retaining left hands the two in the center
   take right hands and all four individuals turn slightly to face in alternate directions.

DAISY CHAIN: The movement is similar to the grand right and left. Starting
   with partner right and left to the next; the dancers then turn back to
   make a right turn with the person behind them. Then forward again with two
   hands, left and right, and back one, right hand. The dancers then progress
   around the set until the original partner is met.

Patter Calls for Series XVI

Heads star thru, pass thru
Star thru, go right and left thru
Swing thru and box the gnat
Go right and left thru
Put the lady in the lead (dixie style)
Make a wave--all eight circulate
Boys do a U turn back--promenade.

Head couples lead to the right and circle to a line
Right and left thru
Do a dixie style to an ocean wave
Girls circulate--boys trade
Left allemande--swing partner--promenade.

Recommended Singing Calls for Series XVI

Sometimes
    Windsor: Number 4897A

Walk Right In
    Flip: Number 118

Worried Man
    Aqua: Number 120

In Your Heart
    Blue Star: Number 1830

CALLS INCLUDED IN SERIES XVII

Flutter wheel
Sweep a quarter
Tag the line

Series XVII

FLUTTER WHEEL: Two couples are facing each other and the ladies start the
figure as if executing a ladies chain. After passing right shoulders the
man takes the lady's left hand in his right hand and walks her back to
place. The result is that the couples are still facing each other with
the lady in her starting position and the man in opposite position.

SWEEP A QUARTER: This call follows the flutter wheel. The couples continue
to move in the line of direction one-quarter more.

TAG THE LINE: The call is executed from any line of four, six, or eight
dancers. The dancers turn to face the center point of the line. Then the
dancers move forward, passing right shoulders with the dancers facing in
the other direction. The dancers will then be given the next directional
call which will tell them which direction to turn, resulting in two equal
lines facing each other.

62

Patter Calls for Series XVII

Head couples square thru--four hands
Do-sa-do the outside two
Star thru
Flutter wheel--
Sweep a quarter
Right and left thru
Dive thru--pass thru
Do-sa-do the outside two
Star thru
Flutter wheel
Sweep a quarter
Right and left thru--dive thru
Star thru
Back out, you're home.

Head couples pair off
Do-sa-do with the outside two
Star thru
Flutter wheel
Sweep a quarter
Right and left thru
Dive thru--star thru
Pass thru--partner trade.

Head couples star thru
Pass thru and do-sa-do with outside two
Star thru--pass thru
Wheel and deal
Double pass thru--first couple go left,
    second couple go right
Flutter wheel and sweep a quarter
Right and left thru
Dive thru--star thru
Back out, you're home.

Head couples flutter wheel
Sweep a quarter and pass thru
Separate and go around one
Into the middle and star thru
Flutter wheel--sweep a quarter
Pass thru--separate go around one
Into the middle and star thru
Back out, you're home.

Head couples slide thru
Pass thru
Star thru
Flutter wheel
Sweep a quarter
Do-sa-do full around
Make an ocean wave
Swing thru--boys trade
Box the gnat
Right and left thru
Dive thru
Star thru--
Back out, you're home.

Head couples pair off
Do-sa-do full around
Make an ocean wave and
Swing thru
Boys run
Tag the line right
Boys trade
Girls run
All eight circulate
Star thru
Crosstrail
Walk by partner--allemande left
    corner
Right to partner for a right and left grand
Meet partner and promenade.

Recommended Singing Calls for Series XVII

Abilene
    MacGregor: Number 2106 B

Series XVIII

EIGHT CHAIN THRU: Two sets of couples are facing each other. The couples travel up one side of the line and down the other, ending back in their original positions. Dancers begin by giving right hands to the person in front, pull-by. Then these dancers facing out do a courtesy turn at the same time the dancers in the center join left hands and pull-by. This call can be done any number of hands: eight chain one, two, three, four, five, six, seven, or eight chain thru.

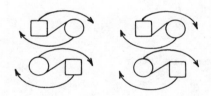

CATCH ALL EIGHT: Couples are facing each other and join right forearms. The couples turn in the direction they are facing for only two steps, then each person executes a half-face turn as they exchange to a left forearm turn. The couples then turn counterclockwise two or more steps, as determined by the caller.

Patter Calls for Series XVIII

One-three star by the left
Corner do-sa-do--full around
Eight chain thru
Count eight hands--meet the corner do-sa-do
Allemande left--promenade

One-three star thru--California twirl
Do-sa-do around the corner
An eight chain thru
Corner do-sa-do
Allemande left--promenade.

All promenade--one-three wheel around
Do a right and left thru
Star thru and do an eight chain five
Your corner do-sa-do
Allemande left corner--swing partner
Promenade home.

Heads right and left thru
Star thru and pass thru
Eight chain thru
Do a right and left thru
Outside two whirl a half sashay
Allemande left--promenade.

Four ladies chain--three-quarters round
One-three wheel around
Right and left thru--turn her
Star thru--eight chain four
Corner do-sa-do
Allemande left the corner--promenade home.

Promenade--heads wheel around
Do a right and left thru
Star thru--start an eight chain thru
Meet those same two--pass thru
Allemande left corner--do-sa-do partner
Swing your partner--promenade home.

Allemande left corner
Right to partner and catch all eight
    A right hand halfway around; back by the left;
    go all the way around; a right to corner and pull-by
And allemande left with corner
Go right and left grand--promenade.

Head couples square thru four hands
Eight chain thru
Right and left thru
Dive thru--pass thru
Eight chain thru
Right and left thru
Dive thru--star thru
Back out, you're home.

Recommended Singing Calls for Series XVIII

Can't Help Believing
    Wagon Wheel: Number 120

Gonna Raise a Ruckus
    Windsor: Number 4818

Hello My Baby
    MacGregor: Number 1008A

Just a Little Lovin
    Windsor: Number 4889

L-O-V-E
    Blue Star: Number 1859

Pickle Up a Doodle
    Windsor: Number 4823

Rolling Along
    Kalox: Number LH 4827

Sally Was a Good Ole Girl
    Wagon Wheel: Number 307

Sweet Thang
    Jewel: Number J-141

Tico Tico
    Kalox: Number 1017

Wishing
    Sets In Order: Number 119A

Series XIX

CAST OFF: From a line of four dancers facing away from the center of the set, the two center people separate and move forward as a couple with the outside person. The outside person acts as a pivot and turns in place.

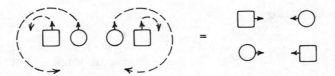

CENTERS IN: Two couples are facing in the same direction with one behind the other. The couple standing behind moves up and stands between the couples in front. The couple in front have moved apart.

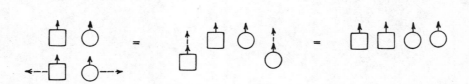

CENTERS OUT: Two couples are facing in the same direction with one behind the other. The couple standing behind moves up and stands on the outside of the couple in front.

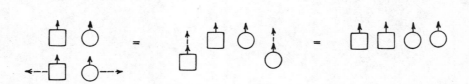

68

FOLD: In any line containing two or more dancers, those indicated move forward and turn to face the person formerly standing beside them.

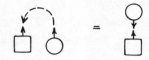

Patter Calls for Series XIX

Heads lead right and circle
Break and make a line of four
Pass thru in front of you--cast off three-quarters round
Then circle up eight
The heads star thru in the middle--pass thru
Left allemande--swing and promenade.

Head couples pair off
Do-sa-do with the outside two
Right and left thru--full turn around
Centers square thru
Outsides cloverleaf
Centers in
Cast off three-quarters
Slide thru
Left allemande the corner
Promenade partner.

Heads pair off and do a right and left thru
Dive thru
Turn thru
Left turn thru with the outside two
Centers square thru three hands
Centers in
Cast off three-quarters
Box the gnat
Pull-by
Allemande left
Right to partner for a right and left grand
Promenade.

Head ladies chain
Head couples crosstrail and
    hook on the ends
Cast off three-quarters
Ends fold and pass thru
Wheel and deal
Centers pass thru
Centers in
Cast off three-quarters
Ends fold
Allemande left and promenade.

Heads pair off
Centers in
Cast off--three-quarters
Ends fold double pass thru
Centers in
Cast off three-quarters
Pass thru
Wheel and deal
Centers square thru--three hands
Centers in
Cast off--three-quarters
Ends fold double pass thru
Centers in
Cast off three-quarters
Pass thru
Wheel and deal
Centers square thru--three hands
Allemande left corner
Right to partner for a right and left grand.
Promenade.

Recommended Singing Calls for Series XIX

I'm Walkin'
    Top: Number 25123

Series XX

BARGE THRU: Executed with two lines of four facing each other. The two
lines go forward and do a half square thru. The dancers facing inward
do a pass thru while the dancers facing outward do a partner trade. The
call ends in the same formation as an eight chain thru.

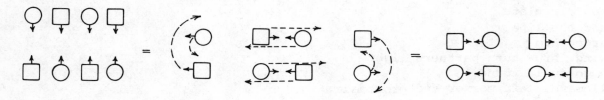

Half Square Thru
Formation

Patter Calls for Series XX

```
Head couples do a half square thru
Circle to a line--side men break
Pass thru
Wheel and deal
Double pass thru
Cloverleaf and substitute
Centers pass thru
Star thru
Pass thru
Partners trade
Barge thru
Allemande left the corner
Promenade.

Head couples crosstrail, go around two
Hook on and make lines of four
Barge thru
Swing thru
Centers run
Couples circulate
Ends circulate
Bend the line
Barge thru
Swing thru--turn partners right
   go full around
Allemande left corner and promenade.
```

Recommended Singing Calls for Series XX

```
No No Nora
   Scope:  Number 527
```

Record Company Bibliography

Airport, Inc.
Alexandria, Louisiana
(Go Records)

Aqua Record Co.
900 Westlake Ave.
Seattle, Washington
(Aqua Records)

Balance Records
P. O. Box 64343
Los Angeles, California
(Balance Records)

Edwards Record Series
P. O. Box 194
Park Ridge, Illinois
(Flip Records)

Golden Square Records
301 Maureen Lane
Pleasant Hills, California
(Golden Square Records)

Grenn, Inc.
P. O. Box 16
Bath, Ohio
(Grenn Records)
(Top Records)

Hi-Hat Records
P. O. Box 69833
Los Angeles, California
(Hi-Hat Records)

Jay-Bar-Kay Records
Box 54
Newtonville, New York
(Jay-Bar-Kay Records)

Jewel Records
Birmingham, Alabama
(Jewel Records)

Kalox Belco Records, Inc.
316 Stau Street
Dallas, Texas
(Kalox Records)

Keeno Records
Leigh, Nebraska
(Keeno Records)

MacGregor Records
729 S. Western Ave.
Los Angeles, California
(MacGregor Records)

Merrbeck Record Series
Houston, Texas
(Blue Star Records)
(Lore Records)
(Bogan Records)

Old Timer Record Co.
P. O. Box 7176
Phoenix, Arizona
(Old Timer Records)

Red Beet Records
College Hills
Greenville, Tennessee
(Red Beet Records)

Scope Records
P. O. Box 64343
Los Angeles, California
(Scope Records)

Sets In Order
462 N. Robertson Blvd.
Los Angeles, California
(Sets In Order Records)

Square Your Sets
P. O. Box 262
Moline, Illinois
(Square Your Sets Records)

Wagon Wheel Record Company
P. O. Box 364
Arvada, Colorado
(Wagon Wheel Records)

Windsor Record Company
5530 Rosemead Street
Temple City, California
(Windsor Records)

After each series, the author gives singing call record suggestions and refers to these records by record title, record company, and record number. This information can be easily found on this Record Company Bibliography for ordering.

Dress, Equipment, and Record Sources

EASTERN AREA

Arizona Fashions
R. R. 1, Box C-311
Lock Haven, Pennsylvania

B & D Western Wear
3509 First Ave. S. W.
Hickory, North Carolina

Berlina Music Store
154 Fourth Avenue
New York, New York 10003

Bill & Val's Carriage House
140 E. Butler Avenue
Chalfont, Pennsylvania

Bob Mason
Box 205
Almand, New York

Buck & Sandy's Western Wear
R. R. 3, Box 80
Fairmont, West Virginia

Calico House
1166 Hooksett Road
Manchester, New Hampshire

Circle C. Western Wear
77 Elm Street
Millbury, Massachusetts

Counts Western Store
4903 Wisconsin Avenue
Washington, D. C.

Dance Record Co.
1159 Broad St.
Newark, New Jersey

Do C Do Shoppe
Church Road & Road 33
Wall, New Jersey

Don's Record
18 Morgan Street
Waterville, Maine

E & D Western Wear
14 Main Street
South Hadley Falls, Massachusetts

Ed & Marea's Square Dance Shop
317 Peninsula Drive.
Erie, Pennsylvania

Educational Activities, Inc.
Box 392
Freeport, New York 11520

Hi-D-Ho Shop
257 Read Street South
Attleboro, Massachusetts

Ironda Square Dance Shoppe
759 Washington Ave.
Rochester, New York 14617

Madelyn Ferrucci Creations
Brewster & Lake Road
Newfield, New Jersey

Marty's Square Dance Shop
404 Cherokee Drive
Greenville, South Carolina

Peg's Square Dance Shop
R. R. 143
Hinsdale, Massachusetts 01235

Petrella's Record Shop
2014 W. Darby Road
Havertown, Pennsylvania

Promenade Shop
Route 106
East Bridgewater, Massachusetts

Ranchland Record Store
R. R. 3
Mechanicsburg, Pennsylvania

Square Dance Shoppe
1828-9 Wylie Ridge Road
Weirton, West Virginia

Sue's Specialty Shop
South Main Street
Topsfield, Massachusetts

Town & Country Square Dance Fashions
3490 Sheridan Drive
Buffalo, New York 14226

SOUTHWESTERN AREA

Amos Square Dance Shop
624 W. Main
Alhambra, California

Callers Supply
P. O. Box 48547
Los Angeles, California

Cee Vee Square Dance Shop
114 S. Western Ave.
Amarillo, Texas

Circle Eight Western Wear
12339 S. Hawthorn
Hawthorn, California

Circle W-J Trading Post
151 W. Elkhorn Ave.
Estes Park, Colorado

Dru Gilmore
P. O. Box 191
Yucaipa, California

Eddie's & Bobbie's
8724 Tonawanda St.
Dallas, Texas

Hill Rancho
15701 S. Crenshow
Gardena, California

Hilton Ardic
1009 A Shary Court
Concord, California

Johnny Velotta Shop
118 S. Lake Street
Los Angeles, California

Judy's Record Store
R. R. 2, Box 191
Denison, Texas

Ka-Mo, Inc.
5001 Douglas Macarty N. E.
Albuquerque, New Mexico

Master Records
P. O. Box 7281
Phoenix, Arizona

Miller Stockman
Box 5407
Denver, Colorado

Modern Radio
424 Valencia Street
San Francisco, California

Nancy Sealey's Record Store
706 B Nimity
China Lake, California

Nita Smith
113 Walton Drive
College Station, Texas

Patio Square Dance Shop
810 E. Pacific Coast Highway
Long Beach, California

Phil Mason's Folk Shop
1531 Clay Street
Oakland, California

Recordland
4457 E. Thomas
Phoenix, Arizona

Rex Old Square Dance Shop
3968 A Studebaker
Long Beach, California

Robertson Dance Shop
3600 - 33rd Ave.
Sacramento, California

Square Dance Records
8575 W. Colfax St.
Denver, Colorado

Square Dance Record Store
8512 LaJolla Court
Ft. Worth, Texas

Vivian Porter Western Wear
1320 E. Highland Ave.
San Bernadino, California

Western Tack & Togs
411 W. Carpenter Freeway
Irving, Texas

MIDWESTERN AREA

Allemande Shop
250 N. Main Street
Crown Point, Indiana

Arrowhead Trading Post
4433 N. Washington Avenue
Royal Oak, Michigan

B-Bar-B Square Dance Shop
315 Main Street
Rochester, Michigan

B-Bar-B Western Wear
1538 Main Street
Speedway, Indiana

Belt & Buckle Western Wear
32380 Center Ridge Road
Ridgeville, Ohio

Buckboard Western Shop
R. R. 2
Marshall, Michigan

C-Bar-L Saddlery
R. R. 3
Valparaiso, Indiana

Cross Trail Record Shop
12130 Center Road
Bath, Michigan

Dancer's Corral
2228 Wealthy S. E.
Grand Rapids, Michigan

Dee's Square Dance Shop
8551 N. Riverview Drive
Kalamazoo, Michigan

Double-O Ranchwear
1460 National Street
Memphis, Tennessee

Dudes & Dolls Shop
5628 E. Washington St.
Indianapolis, Indiana

Gilbert's Mexican Shop
15 East Market Street
Akron, Ohio

Happy Valley
15113 Stanwood S. W.
Dalton, Ohio

Jimco
6210 S. Webster
Fort Wayne, Indiana

Maxine's Square Dance Shop
4428 S. 7th Street
Terre Haute, Indiana

Midwest Radio Company
3414 W. North Ave.
Milwaukee, Wisconsin

Mission Record Shop
5908 Woodson Road
Mission, Kentucky

Nick's Western Shop
245 E. Market
Kingsport, Tennessee

Parker Studio
Highway 3
Kendallville, Indiana

Raceway Saddlery
406 Thomas Avenue
Forest Park, Illinois

Ruthad Petticoats and Pants
8869 Avis Street
Detroit, Michigan

Square Dance Shoppe
28933 Euclid Avenue
Wickliffe, Ohio

Stevens Camera Shop
3600 S. Main Street
Elkhart, Indiana

Wichita Western Store
1018 W. 31st Street
Wichita, Kansas

SOUTHERN AREA

Chez Bea Square Dance Shop
650 N. E. 128th Street
North Miami, Florida

Cross-Trail Square Dance Shop
4150 S. W. 70th Court
Miami, Florida

Dance Ranch
Carrollton Shopping Center
New Orleans, Louisiana

Dance Records
P. O. Box 11776
Atlanta, Georgia

Do-Sal Shoppe
1103 Crysler South
Independence, Missouri

Gordon Brothers
2488 Palm Ave.
Hialeah, Florida

Keith Clothing Shop
301 19th Street
Birmingham, Alabama

Pioneer Shop
306 Camp Street
New Orleans, Louisiana

Record-Rac
1607 Peachtree Circle North
Jacksonville, Florida

Square Dance Corral
2435 Dixie Highway
Wilton Manor, Florida

The Square Dance Shop
75 S. Palm Street
Saratoga, Florida

NORTHWESTERN AREA

Armeta
12505 N. E. Fremont Street
Portland, Oregon

Deckers Records
East 3936 17th Street
Spokane, Washington

Gateway Records
10013 N. E. Wasco Avenue
Portland, Oregon

Kappies Record Store
10400 Renton Ave. South
Seattle, Washington

Schleunings Record Store
R. R. 2, Box 15
Rapid City, South Dakota

Square Dance Distributors
204 Lyric Bldg.
Omaha, Nebraska

Western Dance Distributors
1230-1/2 Westlake Avenue North
Seattle, Washington

Book and Magazine Bibliography

1. American Association of Health, Physical Education, and Recreation, Materials for Teaching Dance (Folk Dance & Square Dance), 1201 16th Street N. W.; Washington, D. C. 20036

2. *American Squares*, 1159 Broad Street, Newark, New Jersey.

3. *Caller's Guide,* Square Dance Callers' Association of Southern California, P. O. Box 1024, South Gate, California.

4. Domon, S. Foster. *The History of Square Dancing*. Barre: Barre Gazette, 1957.

5. Hall, J. Tillman. *Dance! A Complete Guide to Social, Folk, and Square Dancing*. Belmont, California: Wadsworth Publishing Company, 1963.

6. Harris, Jane, Anne Pittman, and Marlys S. Waller. *Dance a While*. Minneapolis: Burgess Publishing Company, 1964.

7. Jensen, Clayne, and Mary Bee Jensen. *Square Dancing*. Salt Lake City, Utah: Brigham Young University Press, 1973.

8. Kraus, Richard. *Square Dances of Today and How to Call Them*. New York: A. S. Barnes and Company, 1950.

9. Phillips, Patricia A. *Contemporary Square Dance*. Dubuque, Iowa: Wm. C. Brown Company Publishers, 1968.

10. Sets In Order, 462 North Robertson Blvd., Los Angeles, California, Offers the following list of publications: *Story of Square Dancing; Record Party Handbook; Square Dance Party Fun; Club Organization Handbook; Indoctrination Handbook; Basic Movements of Square Dance.*

11. Shaw, Lloyd. *Cowboy Dances*. Caldwell, Idaho: The Caxton Printers, 1939.

12. Shaw, Lloyd. *The Round Dance Book*. Caldwell, Idaho: The Caxton Printers, 1948.

13. *Training Manual,* Square Dance Callers' Association of Southern California, P. O. Box 1024, South Gate, California.

Square Dance Associations

ALABAMA
Tennessee Valley Square Dance Association
4113 Nelson Drive N. W.
Huntsville, Alabama   35810

ALASKA
Alaska Federation of Square Dance Clubs
P. O. Box 121
Juneau, Alaska   99801

ARIZONA
Associated Square Dance Club of Arizona
2650 N. 41st Street
Phoenix, Arizona   85008

ARKANSAS
Arkansas State Square Dance Federation
William Lisko
Des Arc, Arkansas   72040

CALIFORNIA
California State Council
1538 Crestline Drive
Santa Barbara, California   93105

COLORADO
Colorado State Square Dance Association
731 Manitou Blvd.
Colorado Springs, Colorado   80904

CONNECTICUT
Connecticut Association of Square Dance
    Clubs
472 Clark Road
Orange, Connecticut   06477

D.C. AREA
Washington Area Square Dance Co-op
    Association
321 Scott Drive
Silver Spring, Maryland   20904

FLORIDA
Florida Federation of Square Dance Clubs
7740 S. W. 65 Place
South Miami, Florida   33143

GEORGIA
Dixie Federation of Square Dance
1821 S. Magnolia Drive
Tallahassee, Florida   32301

HAWAII
Hawaii Federation of Square Dance
    Clubs
P. O. Box 1
Pearl City, Hawaii   96782

IDAHO
Idaho Federation of Square Dance
    Clubs
Box 21
Fort Hall, Idaho

ILLINOIS
Illinois Federation of Square Dance
    Clubs
2444 South 7th Street
Springfield, Illinois   62703

INDIANA
Indiana Dancers Association
407 South 4th Avenue
Beech Grove, Indiana   46107

IOWA
Iowa State Federation of Square
    Dance Clubs
826 25th Street N. E.
Cedar Rapids, Iowa   52402

KANSAS
Heart of America Federation of Square
    Dance
4021 W. 97th Street
Overland Park, Kansas   66207

KENTUCKY
Kentuckiana Square Dance Association
920 Iola Road
Louisville, Kentucky   40207

LOUISIANA
Louisiana Square Dance Association
833 S. Burgess Drive
Baton Rouge, Louisiana   70815

MAINE
Cumberland County Recreation Council
20 Noyes Street
Portland, Maine   04103

MARYLAND
Mason Dixon Square Dance Federation
3018 Woodside Avenue
Baltimore, Maryland 21234

MASSACHUSETTS
Eastern District Square Dance
Association
811 Matianuck Avenue
Windsor, Massachusetts 06095

MICHIGAN
Michigan Council of Square Dance
Clubs
878 Woodside Drive
Muskegon, Michigan 49441

MINNESOTA
Square Dance Federation of Minnesota
383 Norseman Court
Rochester, Minnesota 55901

MISSOURI
Heart of America Federation of Square
Dance
R. R. #1
Peculiar, Missouri 64078

MONTANA
Montana Federation of Square Dance
P. O. Box 66
Troy, Montana 59935

NEBRASKA
Nebraska Square Dance Association
1316 Quince Street
Sidney, Nebraska 69162

NEVADA
Nevada State Square Dance Association
4722 Galsam Street
Las Vegas, Nevada 89108

NEW JERSEY
Federation of Del. Square Dance Clubs
170 Swedesboro Road
Gibbstown, New Jersey 08027

NEW MEXICO
New Mexico State Square Dance Association
1205 Stull St.
Las Cruces, New Mexico 88001

NEW YORK
Capital District Square Dance
Association
1445 Via Del Mar Road
Schenectady, New York 12309

NORTH CAROLINA
Folk and Square Dance Federation of
North Carolina
906 Lewis Street
Fayetteville, North Carolina 28203

NORTH DAKOTA
North Dakota Square Dance Clubs
Marv Enoos
Hunter, North Dakota 58408

OHIO
Ohio State Corporation of Square Dance
Clubs
R. R. #2
Bluffton, Ohio 45817

OKLAHOMA
Oklahoma State Federation of Square
Dance Clubs
2704 S. W. 48th Street
Oklahoma City, Oklahoma 73119

OREGON
Oregon Federation of Square Dance
Clubs
250 Fifth Street
Madras, Oregon 97741

PENNSYLVANIA
Allegheny Valley Square Dance Association
220 Brusses Street
St. Mary's, Pennsylvania 15857

RHODE ISLAND
Rhode Island Federation of Square
Dance Clubs
209 Maryland Ave.
Greenville, R. I. 02888

SOUTH CAROLINA
South Carolina Square Dance Federation
404 Cherokee Drive
Greenville, South Carolina 29607

SOUTH DAKOTA
South Dakota Square Dance Federation
1724 S. First Street
Aberdeen, South Dakota   57401

TENNESSEE
Tennessee Valley Square Dance
    Association
6510 Cedar Point Road
Huntsville, Alabama   35811

TEXAS
Heart of Texas Square Dance Association
P. O. Box 825
Kileen, Texas   76541

UTAH
Association of Square Dance Clubs of
    Utah
446 South 200 East
Farmington, Utah   84035

VERMONT
Mountain Valley Square Dance Association
P. O. Box 26
Vernon, Vermont   05354

VIRGINIA
Peninsula Square Dance Association
105 Springs Road
Yorktown, Virginia   23490

WASHINGTON
Square Dance Federation of Washington
P. O. Box 324
Royal City, Washington   99357

WEST VIRGINIA
Kanawha Valley Square Dance Council
723 Gordon Drive
Charleston, West Virginia   25303

WISCONSIN
Square Dance Association of Wisconsin
2522 Barbara Avenue
Appleton, Wisconsin   54911

WYOMING
Big Horn Basin Square Dance Federation
953 Hobson Road
Lander, Wyoming   82520